Social Media Marketing

for Small Businesses

How to Get New Customers,
Make More Money, and
Stand Out From the Crowd

For permission requests & bulk order purchase options, email
support@smmfsb.com

First Print Edition 2022.
Aude Publishing

Hardcover ISBN 978-1-957470-08-5
Paperback ISBN 978-1-957470-07-8
eISBN 978-1-957470-09-2
LLCN 2022919196

Social Media

Marketing

for Small Businesses

How to Get New Customers, Make More Money, and
Stand Out From the Crowd

Jon Law

Aude Publishing

so·cial

···
sō'shəl

    1. of or relating to human society and its modes of organization.

me·di·a

···
ˈmiː.di.ə
    1. an organized source of information.

Contents

Social Media Marketing

for Small Businesses

How to Get New Customers,
Make More Money, and
Stand Out From the Crowd

1

Why go social?

Social media has erupted onto the global scene as the now-dominant medium of connection and collaboration. For people and society at large, the implications of this transformation are massive. For businesses, they are even more profound. Commerce in the modern globalized and digitalized ecosystem relies upon a toolset comprised of strategies and opportunities not available mere decades ago. While new challenges have emerged, the latent potential constrained within small businesses has more of an opportunity than ever to explode upon a competitive landscape no longer limited by geography.

The idea of writing this book first came to mind when a friend showed me the books she was reading to learn how to market her small business on social media. I was astounded by the abject lack of complete and up-to-date information; these books were preaching apps that became irrelevant years ago, advertising strategies that stopped at Facebook Ads, and social media advice that boiled down to "be yourself."

Following these observations, I decided to write a book that helps small business owners grow their businesses through the experiences I've had in building dozens of small businesses to social influence spanning a quarter-billion views and millions of followers, which directly translated to millions in sales, stronger bottom lines, and many more customers.

Why is incorporating digital and social media marketing into your business strategy so important? This is a fair question—one often ignored by those preaching some free-for-all fantasy of the social media and digital landscape for business—and one that comes down to fundamental shifts in the global business environment.

Our analysis must begin with the understanding that digitalization has been the defining characteristic of the 21st-century business world. The internet has removed geographic barriers, incurred mass availability of knowledge, and provided an unprecedented degree of opportunity to anyone with a digital device and connection. As more of the world moves online, digitalization must either be a prime determinant in your business—assuming some degree of physicality—or, as with purely digital businesses, the dominating determinant.

However, while digitalization has opened the door to opportunity, it has also created a much more competitive environment. As opposed to competition being relatively constrained as per geographic proximity (though it may be for your physical business, the same rules do not apply when working digitally), such limits have largely been erased. A small business selling customized pillows in California competes against online pillow sellers in New York and Canada, while a software business based out of Japan competes with Cape Town and London startups. As a business operating in this kind of environment, you must not just understand the landscape of the digital world, but learn to thrive in it.

Largely as a result of digitalization, globalization has further interconnected the world's economies to an unprecedented extent.

We're all literally in this together, and globalization plays into all digital strategies. The combination of digitalization and globalization has incurred not only greater and fiercer competition but also connected a wide range of markets and introduced the possibility of serving niche markets which now collectively offer enough demand to sustain large-scale business. These two trends play into the increased role that outsourcing plays in labor and business. Outsourcing reduces overhead and increases the value of expert *leveragers* of the digital age, versus those playing by outdated rules.

Many businesses, especially online-only businesses, can reap ample rewards by expanding into non-native countries. One such example is this book, and the others managed by my agency—nearly 60% of our sales come from outside the US even though most of the books we sell are purchased in English.

These are just some reasons as to why digital and social marketing have burst onto the scene, and why countless businesses are shifting toward the opportunities present in these fields.

I am not attempting to sugarcoat the realities of a complex and rapidly changing competitive environment. Digital and social media marketing will not be life-changing for every business. Rather, every business can benefit from a variety of low-hanging opportunities present in the digital space, while for a good chunk, the strategies presented in this book will indeed be game changers.

We now understand the importance of going social. In the interest of ground-up understanding, what exactly is social media?

2

Social What-now?

A book about social media marketing must first answer the question of what exactly social media is—yes, kids today seem to always be on it, while some swear by its negative effects, but what truly is it?

Social mediums are best defined as online communities that allow users to interact with each other. In this manner, it is quite an expansive field—just think of each time you text a group chat on your phone, scroll through Wikipedia, or view a post shared by an old friend. In all these cases, people are interacting with each other on the Internet—this is what social media fundamentally means.

Social media marketing isn't just about posting videos or paying influencers. It's about leveraging the ways in which people interact online to get your products and services into more hands. This ties back to the question of whether going social is even worthwhile—in fact, it's imperative to go social because social media is the type of interaction that the modern world is predicated upon.

Today, the most popular social media applications operate on a UGC, or user-generated content, system. UGC means that people using a given website or app (such as Facebook or YouTube) create content that other users engage with, and so forth, in an endlessly cyclical manner. Because of UGC, all the most popular social networking sites are free and rely upon selling advertisements to make money. In this way, social networking websites only continue to exist because of businesses that choose to advertise with them. The very fact that businesses continue to advertise on social applications means that advertising continues to be a viable business strategy, while the explosions in the content creation and influencer marketing industries speak to the viability of content as a business strategy.

As stated, this book aims to provide a comprehensive guide to digital and social media marketing for small businesses. It is first being published in the fall of 2022 and will update each year to reflect the rapidly changing fields and opportunities it explores. It will mold itself to the feedback delivered by actual small business owners. To provide such feedback and advice for future entrepreneurs as you and your business progress using the methods and strategies present in this book, please shoot us an email concerning both what worked and what didn't, or with questions, to team@smmfsb.com.

Looking forward, we have split the text into two high-level parts. It builds out a conceptual strategic framework in the first four chapters. It then continues with a detailed exploration of social media marketing, social advertising, content creation, and related subjects encompassed within the grander sphere of digital marketing.

This book has been written specifically with small business owners and entrepreneurs in mind. Small businesses and their owners form the backbone of all economic activity and should not find themselves limited competitively due to a lack of knowledge. That is the driving purpose behind this text. I pray it does you justice.

3

Start with Strategy

Hard work is only half the equation; smart work is the other half. Likewise, growing your business through digital means is just as much about knowing what to do as how to do it. Even the best-executed digital strategies fail if applied to sub-optimal platforms or, even worse, if designed to hit the wrong objectives.

These reasons are why such an emphasis is placed on strategy throughout this book. We'll get to execution, and all the on-the-ground tips and tricks—but trust me in that high-level thinking is where any successful business, operating in any field or realm, begins.

Three levels make up the strategy profile of your business: brand strategy, digital strategy, and social strategy. While the overarching focus of this book is on the latter two, we'll walk through all three levels to ensure your business begins with strong groundwork.

Brand Strategy

Brand strategy is all about identity. It explores the questions of what your business is, why it exists, and what it's trying to achieve. Nailing down your brand strategy ensures you can powerfully communicate your brand, which will help you reach your target customers and grow your business.

First, what is a brand? We view your brand as the way people (including you) view your business. Brand strategy is about messaging that imbues potential customers with a favorable view of your business: before sharing that message, however, you need to make sure it both accurately represents your business and makes sense from a marketing perspective.

To create your brand strategy, ask yourself the following questions. It is recommended that you articulate your thoughts in a journal or otherwise expansive space:

1. Who is your business for? What's the problem it solves, or needs and wants it meets?

2. Why should customers come to you versus competitors? Are you cheaper, higher quality, or better for the environment? What's your mission, and what are your values?

3. How do you want your business to feel? You may find this to be a strange exercise, but try it out—imagine the personality, tone, and vibe of the business as if it were a person.

These questions fulfill the conceptual portion of brand strategy, which may be thought of as your brand essence—simply put, it is what makes your business what it is. Add some substance to these ideas in the following steps:

1. Create an elevator pitch for your business in a few
    sentences.

2. Choose a few strong taglines that communicate the purpose
    of your business.

3. If you haven't already, ensure you've thought out the color
    scheme, logo, and typography that best represents your
    business.

In taking these steps, you should have a much clearer idea, or at
least one that is physically written down, of what your business is
and how you can best communicate it to the world.

   With this step completed, we can move on to digital
strategy and social strategy.

Digital Strategy

Digital strategy is an art of absolutes: with your brand messaging
and identity clearly defined, the creation of your digital strategy is
more about the actual digital methods and principles you will use to
grow your business.

   Digital strategy, as with all proper strategies, begins with
goals. A second oft-forgotten piece must also be incorporated, that
being clarity on the actual key performance indicators (KPIs) used to
measure progress toward digital goals.

   To identify the objective of your digital strategy, start with
the high-level goal of your business. Are you trying to make the
most money possible? Are you less interested in growth, and would

rather prioritize stability? Or are you trying to reach the most people possible?

Take some time to consider it (be honest with yourself!) and write it down in one sentence.

That sentence forms the basis of your entire digital strategy. A major mistake of most businesses in entering the digital space is that they do it with their eyes closed—on some notion of keeping up with the times but with no idea as to why they're there, these businesses will ultimately fail to fully exploit the range of digital tools available to them as per their lack of cohesion.

It's not just about having an objective—once yours is identified, work backward to specify the key social metrics you will use to measure your progress toward that goal. Here are some of the most common metrics employed by businesses to measure their digital success:

Views: if your goal is putting as many eyes on your business as possible, views are what it's all about.

Sales Calls: if your business onboards clients through calls, the number of calls (or clients) generated digitally is a great metric to consider.

Return on Ad Spend (ROAS): if your business uses ads, ROAS is the principal metric to determine the profitability of ads.[1]

---

[1] ACOS (advertising cost of sales) is used on some platforms.

Meetings Booked: if your business operates out of a physical location, the number of meetings booked online may be your principal measure of success.

Units sold: if your business sells products online, the more units sold, the better!

The above list may not include a metric that fits your business model. If that's the case, start with your goal and ask yourself the question "what does my business need more of to hit its goals?"

Whatever your answer is, it's likely to be the metric that your brand strategy is built around.

Most businesses operating online don't have this critical piece in place: they measure success by the number of followers or views they get, despite those flashy numbers not reflecting how successful the digital strategy of the business is, nor considering the metrics that meaningfully contribute to its vision and goals. Take a moment now to write down your KPI.

As part of your digital strategy, you're now clear on what you're trying to gain and how you'll measure success. The next step is determining which platforms, methods, and strategies optimally contribute to the realization of your KPI.

Note that two general buckets of digital strategies exist: paid marketing and organic marketing. Paid marketing consists of digital advertising (which comes in many forms—think TV ads versus sponsored search results). Organic marketing mostly concerns social presence establishment as a first step, followed by content creation, and drives traffic to your business without directly paying for traffic or leads.

Before making a decision on what's best for your business, note that great digital strategies incorporate elements of both organic and paid digital marketing, often in an intertwined manner (e.g., advertising to help organic content perform better). Also, consider that it's usually best to experiment with each, as you'll never really know what could have been a game-changer unless you've tried. Thankfully, most ad platforms make experimenting low-cost and lower-effort.

While incorporating elements of each is optimal, here are the profiles of businesses that are best served by each overarching digital strategy:

Paid digital marketing: nearly every business can be served by some type of online advertisement.

Ads targeted geographically work best for businesses operating out of a physical location, such as mom-and-pop shops or technology retailers.

Ads targeted towards interests, as well as sponsorships and influencer marketing (all of which we'll explore), work best for businesses offering products or services that can be purchased online, such as an artist selling nature prints or an online tutor.

Organic digital marketing: again, most businesses can benefit from some type of organic digital marketing. At a basic level, all businesses should ensure that information about them is available online (something we'll thoroughly cover in the next section) and establish an email list that allows them to reach customers with news, business updates and launches, and any other relevant information.

At a second tier of organic marketing, any business that benefits from increased community engagement should regularly share content that attracts and grows its community (online or offline). We'll get into the types and processes of content creation further on.

At a final tier of organic marketing, businesses that sell products or services online should regularly create content designed to grow an audience and convert it into paying customers. This entire concept of funnel-building will be examined at length.

With all this in mind, take a moment to consider and write down the digital strategies that will best serve your business.

By now, you should have a clear idea of the objective you're trying to hit, the KPI that best serves the objective, and the best digital strategy to maximize that KPI. These steps get you to a good place in terms of digital vision and strategy for your business.

While reading from here on out, keep both your brand strategy and digital strategy in the back of your head as the big-picture framework to be filled in by all the info coming up.

Social Strategy

Social media strategy completes the final level of our digital strategy pyramid. It involves the establishment of a business's social presence, social platforms on which the business should post content, and content strategy. You'll establish a social media strategy for your business through the MAGIC system: goals, audience, medium, content, and implementation.

Goals and **audience** have already been introduced throughout the brand strategy and digital strategy exercises. Do take some time to build upon them, especially when it comes to defining your audience. Expand your thinking of whom your business serves by identifying your target demographic (the people you're trying to reach) and their interests. These are the profiles you will use to design social content and target customers on paid advertising platforms.

Additionally, make sure that your digital strategy KPI makes sense in a social media context. For example, "views" transfers over easily as a KPI since it's utilized in a digital and social context, but something like "online bookings" is more measurable as "link clicks" since clicks on links embedded in social media profiles is the direct action on a social media platform that leads to the overarching KPI.

In this manner, consider the steps you want customers to take, and consider the last step you want customers to take on a social media platform. This, in essence, is the KPI of your business within the context of social media.

Next, consider the social **mediums**, or platforms, through which you can best meet your social strategy KPI. Some of the platforms we'll be exploring merely require your business to have a presence through an inactive or semi-active profile. This bucket of platforms does not require content created specifically for them unless your business fits the niche of the platform (take Pinterest and design-focused businesses). The first four platforms we're looking at (beyond the website, which is an absolute requirement) are general purpose and require specialized content should you recognize them as a valuable social medium for your business. The next two are less important but are still great (and ultimately profitable) to build on. The final two require profiles, but don't need specialized content unless that fits into your MAGIC plan.

I cannot stress the importance of having a social presence set up across all of these platforms. This step of the MAGIC plan is rather where you should decide on which platforms you will commit your business to post content and actively pursue growth.

Website: your website is the digital face and hub of your business. It provides an easy way for customers to learn about your business and capture any information they could possibly need. It's also an opportunity for you to sell products or services online, post content, build an email list, and direct viewers toward your other digital profiles. In sum, all businesses absolutely must have a quality website in our modern day and age.

Instagram: Instagram is one of the most embedded and multi-faceted social media platforms. It began as a photo-sharing platform but has expanded to include a multitude of content types through Instagram reels (short-form video, or under one minute in length), Instagram videos (long-form video, or over one minute in length), stories (disappearing photo/video content), Instagram shopping, and Instagram live. Many businesses can list their products directly within the Instagram app. Regardless, producing content on Instagram is a must-do for nearly all small businesses, whether your goal is to build an audience or connect with local communities.

Facebook: Facebook was the first social media service beyond blogs to hit mainstream usage. Like Instagram, multiple types of content can be shared, including text, photo, video, and livestreams. Facebook is a must-do for all small businesses.

Google: your Google business profile is how Google users (which is everyone) can quickly get information about your business through search engines like Chrome and Google Maps. Yelp functions in a similar manner to Google Business Profiles, and while not covered henceforth, consider following the outline presented in the upcoming Google Business profile setup section to claim your Yelp page at business.yelp.com.

YouTube: YouTube is the quintessential video-sharing website consisting mostly of long-form videos (over ten minutes) as well as short-form videos through YouTube shorts. It is a good place to host a few walkthroughs or introduction videos for your business. On any larger or more consistent scale, producing quality long-form YouTube videos is a high-investment task best for businesses that operate online; take software companies or digital agencies. YouTube shorts, however, are an easy place to share the short-form videos your business makes, if any, for primary distribution on other platforms.

TikTok: TikTok is the dominant player in the short-form space. Its ad platform presents a major opportunity to businesses selling products or services online, while the entirety of the platform is a great way to introduce people at scale to your business and community.

LinkedIn: LinkedIn is the primary networking app for businesses and professionals; all types of content can be shared upon it, and it's a great way for nearly any business (and small business owner!) to make professional connections, recruit talent, and engage with a local audience.

Twitter: Twitter is the classic short-form text-sharing application. It's a great way to post quick updates about your products, services, and business. It's best for businesses not specifically looking to reach a local audience, but rather to reach a wider audience not limited by geography.

Pinterest: Pinterest is a visual photo-sharing platform. It's best for businesses with some sort of physical identity attached to their products or services, such as fashion brands, real estate managers, or the like, as well as any business primarily targeting women (as 85% of Pinterest's 80-odd million users are women).

With these descriptions in mind, take some time to consider the platforms which best serve the maximization of your social goals.

The next step in the MAGIC system is content. This breaks down to the type of content and the regularity of content your business will create and share on the identified platforms. Content breaks down into four possible categories:

Image: this category represents all content that is shared as a still frame, whether product photographs or graphic design images detailing an advertising message.

Video: this category includes both short-form (under one minute in length) and long-form (over one minute in length) video content.

Writing: this category is broad and includes several notable content types: email, blog, and text being the big three.

Audio: though less popular for businesses, audio content primarily consists of podcasts and live, audio-only events.

The type of content you create depends upon the social mediums you chose as those to pursue. Following are the content types present on each described platform:

- Website
    - All content types
- Instagram
    - Photo, video, live
- TikTok
    - Short-form video, live
- Facebook
    - Photo, video, live
- YouTube
    - Video, live
- Twitter
    - Short-from writing
- LinkedIn
    - Writing, video, live

- Pinterest
  - Photo, video

Best practices for content creation are explored further on in the book. For now, write down the content types that your business will be producing and sharing.

At this point, you know what you're aiming at, whom you're producing content for, on which platforms you will share the content, and what form that content will take.

The final step in the MAGIC system is determining **implementation**. Implementation refers to the processes that must be put in place to turn your digital and social strategy into a reality in your business.

This varies drastically as per the type of business: a single entrepreneur running his or her online tutoring business will not work the same as a thirty-person accounting business, for example, when it comes to advertising or content creation. We'll explore ways to maximize the efficiency of processes such as content creation throughout chapter six.

Generally, the systems and practices you'll need to consider when it comes to social media boil down to the following:

Technical Management: who can manage the depths of a WordPress or Shopify website? This is required at a bare minimum during the creation of a website or any other digital process requiring technical knowledge (unless you or your people are willing to learn yourselves) and must be present at some level thereafter to prevent simple technical errors from snowballing into unnecessary impediments (for example, not turning on auto-updates for WordPress plugins and crashing the website as a result).

Content Ideation and Iteration: ideation and creation are best thought of as separate processes. As a long-time influencer, I've found that crunching content ideation and creation into the same window is unnecessarily stressful and nearly always results in lower-quality content. Future content creation must be tied into analytics and the performance of recent content (for example, if a video blows up, produce more videos with a similar style or message, while if a video doesn't perform well, stop producing that kind of content).

Content Creation: this can take many forms, as it consists of content creation across a host of different content types: writing, photo, video, etc.

Scheduling, Posting, and Managing: posting content, responding to comments and messages, updating profiles, and so on. This work is low skill, though it does require some degree of communication ability, as well as knowledge of the business, given its regular interactions with customers.

Budget: many social media processes can be outsourced or automated. Doing so comes with a price tag even apart from the cost of paid advertising. Whether expenses arise from labor or advertising, making sure the digital endeavors of your business are profitable and adjusting corresponding budgets as per such information is a regular process that is important to implement.

While these processes cover most of what your business needs for successful operations, you may need to build out alternative systems to manage other work that comes up. In such cases, aim to automate and streamline whenever possible while maintaining a consistent vision and mission across the board. As a quick tip, keep in mind that young people are often willing to work as unpaid interns when it comes to social media work.

We've now arrived at the end of the MAGIC system. You should have a clear idea of the following:

- What your business is setting out to achieve on social media and in the digital environment.
- The type of people you will reach.
- The platforms on which you will progress.
- The type of content you will create.
- The processes you will implement at your business to make it all happen.

Now, you have completed all three strategic levels. You have clarity in who you are and what you'll do as a business operating online.

What's left is getting it done: the rest of the book is a deep dive into bringing the steps you've outlined into reality, beginning with a guide to setting up a digital presence for your business.

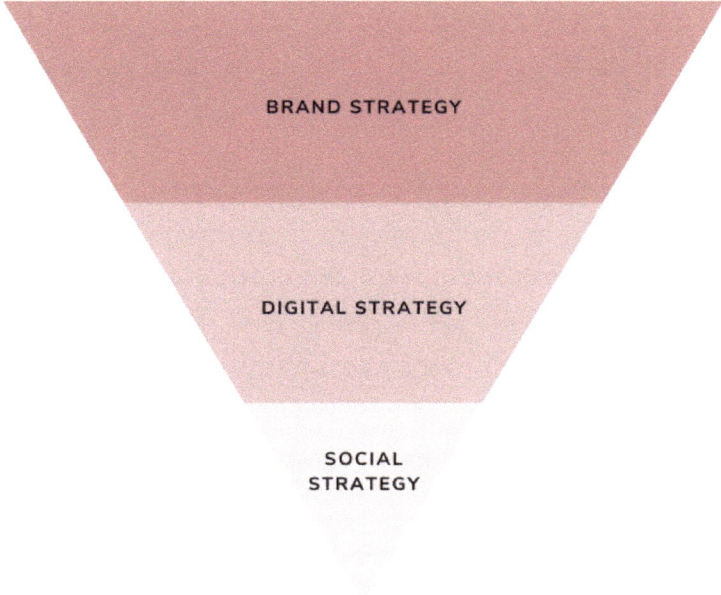

The three levels of strategy.

4

Establishing your Digital Presence

Regardless of content or social media strategy, a necessary step for all small businesses is the establishment of their digital presence through the creation of social profiles across the platforms listed in chapter three. This serves several purposes: it provides greater exposure for the business across search engines, ensures that information can be found about the business, and secures usernames, as well as accounts, for future use.

It's important to set up social profiles in a manner that provides a baseline degree of information about your business to viewers and ranks well in the algorithms. This ensures that if people search for your business or a service/product of the type you provide anywhere online, your profile will come up near the top. Again, regardless of your content strategy, this is an absolute imperative.

Each platform has its own best practices for setting up profiles. Across the board, aim to secure the username that best represents your business. Exclude numbers and underscores whenever possible and mitigate length. Consider a few examples (in red are usernames you wouldn't use, in green are usernames you would use):

Mary'sB&B: mary_bed_breakfast | marysbedandbreakfast | marysbnb
Omni: omninewyork | omni2 | omni_besttech | omni
Wholer Foods: wholerfoods4u | wholer_foods_nyu | wholerfoods

Across the board, you'll need a quality profile photo. You'll typically make this your company logo—just keep in mind that the clearer and less crowded it is, the better. Make sure to customize your logo if it wouldn't otherwise fit in a profile photo setting.

Usernames and profile photos are the cross-platform essentials—following are best practices for setting up social profiles on a per-platform basis, ranked in order of importance: [2]

Google Business

Business Profiles are a service offered by Google to make your business searchable across search engines and map apps. If your business has a physical location, this is an essential first step, and one guaranteed to drive more traffic to your location. Business profiles are also where customers can leave reviews on their experience, which can further serve as social proof to convert digital traffic into real-life customers. As an owner of your business profile, you can answer questions, respond to reviews, set up alerts, enable direct messaging, and publish posts.

---

[2] Across all platforms, attempt to verify your profile. This usually just requires your business to have been featured in articles published by major media organizations. While instructions to get verified vary on a per-platform basis, make sure to inquire as to the process and submit a verification request once your business meets the media requirement.

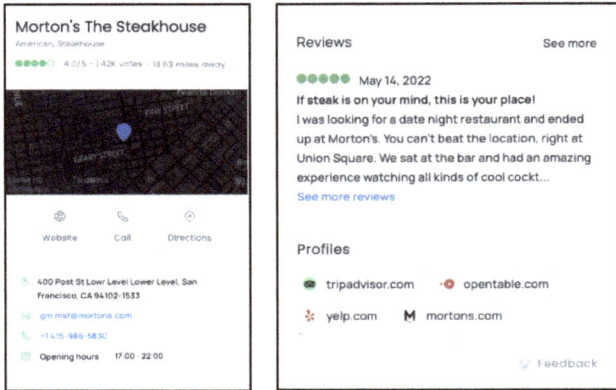

Note this Google Business profile for Morton's Steakhouse, which comes up when locals search "steakhouse" or "steak near me." In this manner, Google Business profiles effectively introduce customers to the restaurant and drive them to the physical location.

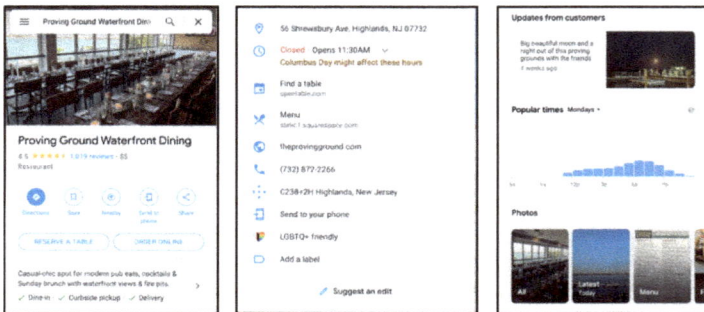

This Google Business profile is searchable on Google Maps. It provides helpful information to potential customers, such as hours, means of contact, popular times, and reservation links.

On Google, business profiles are attached to the physical location, name, and category of the business. Anyone can submit a location for a business profile, meaning that your business may already have a profile. If it does, then you will need to claim the profile and build upon it. If not, you will need to create one for your business.

To claim a profile, first search for your business (through the address or name) on Google maps. Then, click "claim this profile" and follow the instructions.

To create a profile, go to google.com/business and click "manage now." Click "add your business to Google" and fill in the necessary information. This includes the business name, address, service area, business category, and contact details.

Once you've either created or claimed your profile, optimize it to perform well in the search engines through the following steps:

Logo & Description: these are the basics. Add a visually pleasing logo and a description that covers the activities and offerings of the business. Think of the description as an elevator pitch: get the idea and value proposition across in a concise, grammatically correct, and algorithm-friendly manner.[3]

Add Photos and Videos: visual aids add depth, improve legitimacy, and attract attention. Include content that covers the outside of the

---

[3] By algorithm friendly, I mean describe the business and business activities using common keywords and search entries—not the time for big words!

physical business location (if any), the inside, the products or services being offered, and the team.

Contact Details. Add business hours and contact information. To track calls coming from the business profile, add a unique number that is not shown anywhere else.[4]

Acquire and Manage Reviews: incentivize customers in some manner to leave a review or ask regulars and friends to leave reviews. You'll want to assemble at least a few dozen 4.5+ star reviews before social proof is largely achieved. Thereafter, gaining more reviews doesn't need to be a priority. Additionally, take time to respond to reviews, whether positive or negative.

Add Products and Services: this is a dramatically underutilized feature, so take full advantage of it. On the Google My Business (GMB) dashboard, navigate to "products" in the left-hand menu. The products tab lets you add merchandise (both physical and digital) and services directly to your GMB profile (restaurants should add offerings under the popular dishes and menu functions, not through products). This is a powerful tool because listed products can directly rank in search results, thus sending customers your way who search not only for your business or business category but for specific products as well. When listing products and services, make sure your photos are numerous and high-quality. Hiring a

---

[4] While Google My Business does provide call attribution analytics in the Insights Report, it only covers click-to-call mobile devices, not all calls made through that number.

photographer, or working with a hobbyist friend, is more than worth it. As in the Google Business Profile description, try to incorporate keywords into the product name and description (to a reasonable extent—overloading is counterproductive). You have 1000 characters to describe the product, so take full advantage of that space. Additionally, while you aren't required to add pricing information, it's great to do so if your pricing doesn't change often. Finally, choose a call-to-action button that fits your goal; if you sell online, the "order online" button typically performs the best, while if you only sell at a physical location, "learn more" or "buy" is the way to go (these buttons should then redirect to a landing page encouraging customers to physically engage with your business). Using these tips, list products and services at the maximum volume your business allows for, as more listings will only serve to increase rankings and drive more traffic.

Regularly check insights: under analytics in the Google My Business dashboard, you can see the search entries customers are entering to find your business profile, the actions they take once on the profile, and the relative performance of content on the profile. Check these analytics at regular intervals to identify trends in customer interest. Use this information to further optimize your GMB profile, as well as your grander social presence.

Instagram

Setting up an optimized Instagram profile begins with the username. Choose a username and profile picture as per the best practice guidelines on page twenty-two. Pick a category that represents your business and make sure the category is set to public on the profile. Likewise, enter the full name of the business or the business slogan in the "name" section (especially if the name is too long to work as a username) and link your business's homepage in the website section.

Utilize the following structure as a starting point for writing your Instagram description:

- Start with one or two lines that highlight the services or products your business provides and identifies your target audience. Do not make this overly long or wordy: focus on simplicity and clarity.
- Include a call-to-action derived from your digital strategy. Are you trying to get social viewers and followers to your website? Are you trying to get them to set up a call with you, or visit the physical location of your business? Whatever it is, use this line to incentivize or prompt viewers to go down that path.
- If you have a special promotion, offering, or new product/service launching soon, consider putting that into the bio as a line.

- Across the board, incorporate emojis to add color and pizzazz, and incorporate keywords that describe your business and its offerings.

Note the following dos and do-nots:

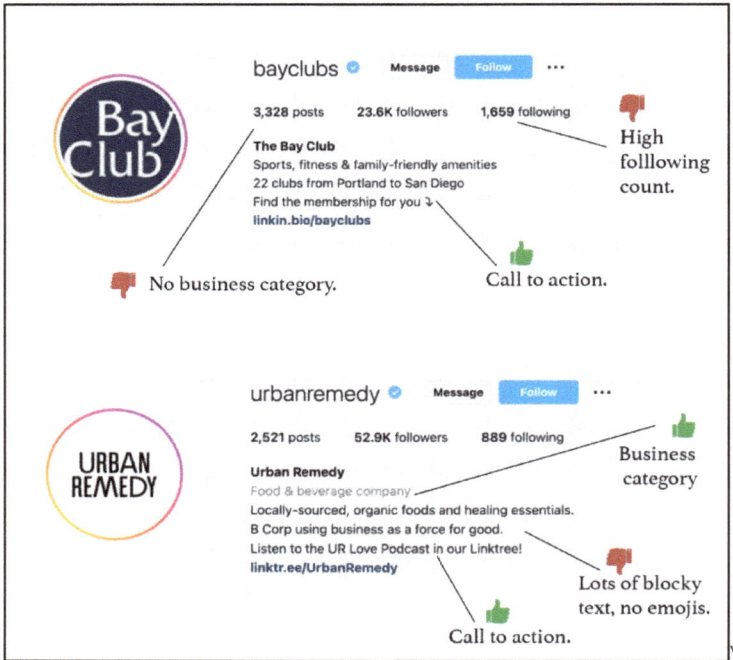

Once your bio is completed, navigate to settings > account > switch to professional account. This transfers your Instagram page from a personal to business account and lets you connect to the associated Facebook account of your business. Business accounts on Instagram have access to post and follower insights, promotions, and profile contact options.

Once the page has migrated to a professional account, add contact options to your profile. It's best to add a phone number, email, and directions to your physical location (if this applies to your business).

These contact options are an important step in converting social viewers and followers on Instagram into customers.

At this point, the Instagram profile of your business should have the following:

- Username.
- Succinct and visually appealing profile photo.
- Business category.
- Business name or slogan (name line).
- Description that introduces the business and associated offerings, states the target audience, and presents a call to action.
- Conversion to a professional account.
- Contact options.

Most of your work is done in terms of actual profile setup. That said, when just starting an account, it's an additional best practice to create a few introductory posts—this ensures that you're not starting out from zero posts when sharing the account. These should provide a base layer of information and content on your business, such as the physical location (if there is one), the team or founders, the website, a nice-looking slide deck, or an event. Publish at least three posts of this type (carousels are best, though not imperative) in accordance with profile creation.[5] Once complete, your business Instagram profile is ready for the world.

---

[5] Carousels refer to Instagram posts containing more than one photo.

LinkedIn

LinkedIn is the dominant social media network for professionals. While it's known for its popularity among the tech community, LinkedIn reaches a vast community of over 800 million members and 58 million registered companies. HubSpot found that LinkedIn is 277% more effective at generating leads than Facebook and Twitter, while 80% of B2B leads come from LinkedIn—for all these reasons and plenty more, LinkedIn is a powerful networking and marketing tool not only for your personal brand but for your business.[6]

Businesses on LinkedIn can create a business page to promote their products or services, post and share content, identify B2B opportunities, increase search presence, and identify job candidates.[7]

To create a LinkedIn business page, you must meet the following requirements:

- Maintain a personal LinkedIn profile for at least seven days, connect with associates, and get a profile strength of at least "intermediate."

---

[6] HubSpot put LinkedIn's visit-to-lead conversion rate at 2.74% versus .77% for Facebook and .69% for Twitter.

[7] Especially through LinkedIn Showcase pages, which are an extension of LinkedIn business pages that emphasize and promote a certain brand or product.

- Maintain a company website and email, and list yourself as a current employee of your business under the "experience" section of your LinkedIn profile.

Then, click the "work" icon in the top right corner of your LinkedIn dashboard and click the "create a company page" button. Choose "small business", fill out the business profile, and click "create page." To fully optimize the page, take these additional steps:

- Add a custom-made cover photo (1584px x 396px). This image should focus on a core element or your business or product and aim to minimize distracting elements.

- Write a summary in the "about" section clearly detailing the story and products or services of your business. Incorporate keywords (as always, to a reasonable extent) into the summary.

- If you have employees, make sure they have personal LinkedIn profiles and list your business as their place of employment. Make sure to add a "follow us on LinkedIn" button to your website.

- If you're looking to hire (or ever find yourself in such a situation), you can attract employees through a career page, which introduces your company history, values, and job opportunities to potential candidates. I can personally vouch for this—I found my first-ever job through LinkedIn.

- Create and join LinkedIn groups. Consider creating a LinkedIn group for your business or a subject relating to the business.

- Leverage the tracking and analytics tools within LinkedIn, primarily the Company Page analytics, to discover how followers are interacting with your page and content (and to garner demographic information).

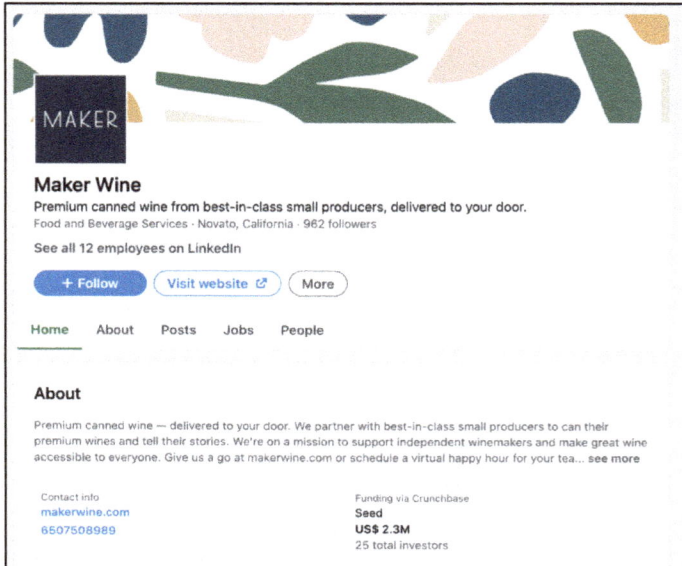

Note that the profile has a lengthy description, contact info, and social-proof funding stats.

These steps ensure that your business will rank organically on major search engines and within LinkedIn. To connect with professionals and businesses within the LinkedIn ecosystem, as well as to publicize new events or offerings, keep in touch with current customers, and drive traffic down the funnel (as discussed further on) it's best to regularly post content on LinkedIn. If you already have a blog on your website, you can easily repurpose content to post on LinkedIn. If not, it may be a good idea to create content yourself, outsource content creation, or work with an intern or other low-cost solution to generate personable content. While we'll get more into the art of minimized-effort and maximized-result content creation in further sections, keep these ideas in the back of your head for now.

Altogether, LinkedIn is the practical requisite for modern-day businesses with a digital presence. While capitalizing upon the professional network available on LinkedIn, make sure to focus not on top-line LinkedIn metrics as a baseline measure of success (views, followers, etc.), but on the degree to which you can introduce viewers to your business, further connections, and acquire long-term customers.

Facebook

Facebook is the largest social media platform in the world by nearly every metric—with 2.91 billion monthly active users, Facebook is a must-have for businesses of all sizes. Establishing your business on Facebook begins with a Facebook page, which is necessary to launch advertisements in addition to capturing the benefit derived from the accumulation of community and social exposure. Facebook business pages are connected to personal Facebook accounts. Once signed into your account, visit facebook.com/pages/creation to set up a business page. Add the page name (the name of your business) and cover photos. Fill in the "about" section with your business details and address, contact information, website, and hours. The following sections constitute your new business page:

Community: this section is usually second only to the homepage in traffic and is where posts, as well as photo and video content, show up. This content can be made by customers, not only the page admins, and offers an opportunity to directly interact with customers.

Events: the events section offers space for you to present and promote upcoming company or community events. You can also invite people to events once created.

Reviews: this tab is where customers can leave reviews on your business and service. Though you can hide the review tab, these reviews do show up at the top of your page, and good reviews are a powerful social proof indicator.

Services: you can fill out this section to provide information on the services your business offers. This includes pricing information.

Shop: under the shop tab, you can engage in e-commerce by directly listing your products. Customers can purchase directly from the page and sales are sent directly to your bank account in an easy foray into e-commerce.

Offers: this section lets you post special deals or discounts and presents a great way to get engagement on your page since customers are incentivized to snag deals as they come up.

Make sure to fill out sections that fit into your digital strategy—for example, if your business can benefit from offering e-commerce to customers, you will leverage the Facebook "shop" page more so than, say, a hair salon. Grow your page organically through content and engage with customers as much as possible.

The utility of Facebook, beyond an ability to create and manage a community, comes from Facebook and Instagram ads. Both are powerful tools to push content to warm users (for example, people in your geographic community, or those most likely to want your products or services) at scale.[8] We'll omit a discussion on these tools now as it's coming up in chapter 8.

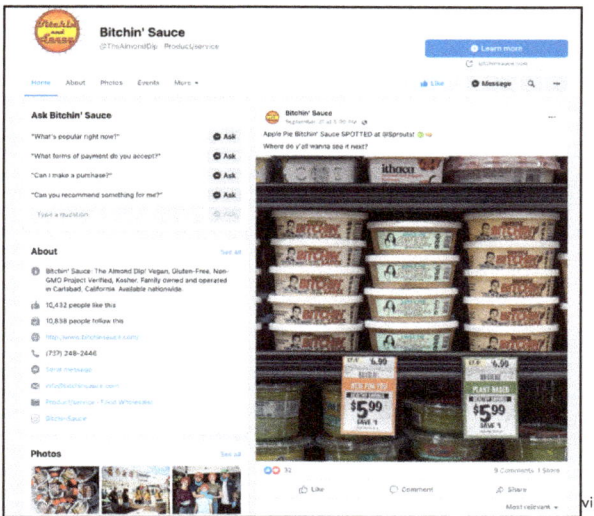

Note how @TheAlmondDip engages its audience through questions, fills out its profile, and regularly shares content.

---

[8] In fact, 75% of brands promote their Facebook posts as per Brandwatch.

Pinterest

Pinterest business accounts offer analytics, ad options, different content types, and early access to new features. To create a business Pinterest account, navigate to business.pinterest.com. Fill out the basic settings and confirm the website of your business. This lets you track the content that people pin from your website and access further cross-platform analytics. Finally, connect your other social accounts to the Pinterest profile, which makes cross-platform content sharing easy, and consider creating some initial boards (as well as buyable pins, depending upon your business).

viii

ix

x

YouTube

YouTube is much more about proper video design versus profile design. Still, the fundamentals are important. When setting up a business YouTube channel, first sign into YouTube through the Gmail account associated with your business. Then, click "my channel" from the dropdown options under the icon in the top right corner of the screen. Click "use a business or other name" in the bottom left and follow the instructions to create a brand account.

Once the brand account is set up, fill in the profile through the channel icon, equivalent to a profile photo, and channel artwork (e.g., the banner image).[9] Then, fill in the channel description—this about section offers much more space than other platforms, so consider copying the "about" text from the website of your business or expanding upon bio text derived from another profile on the business. You can also add a multitude of links in this section. Make sure to link your website, Google business profile, and all other links you consider essential to your business and funnel. Note that social accounts get linked to the banner on your channel's homepage for greater visibility.

Finally, note that YouTube offers space for a "channel trailer" on your channel's homepage. This is the video that is shown to new viewers on your page. It's best to set up this trailer prior to posting other content to ensure maximized conversions. Try to make this video interesting; think of it as a first impression. In this manner, as opposed to a simple introduction to your business's website,

---

[9] Channel icons and banners are respectively sized at 800x800 and 1546x423 pixels.

service, or location, consider a walkthrough of your physical location (if you have one), an interview with team members, a vlog of a CEO's day-in-the-life, or something of the like. An engaging channel trailer, even if you don't regularly produce content on YouTube, goes a long way to promote your YouTube page as a node in your grander social presence.[10]

      In the below examples, note the use of the channel icon and artwork, the social and website links in the bottom right of the artwork banner, and the engaging channel trailer.

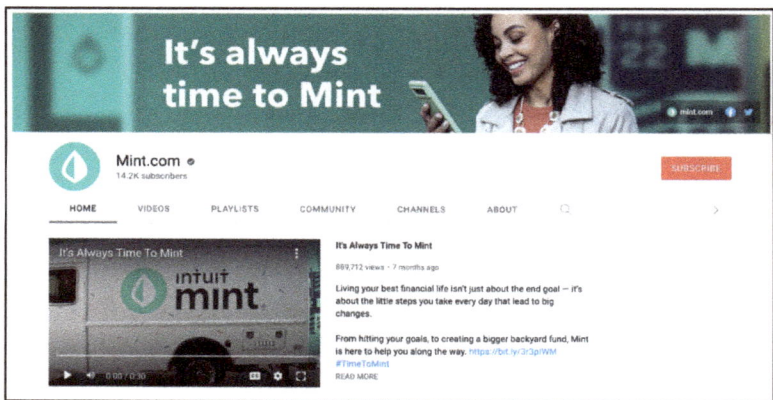

xi

---

[10] You'll also set up playlists and various channel sections if or when your business begins to create content on YouTube.

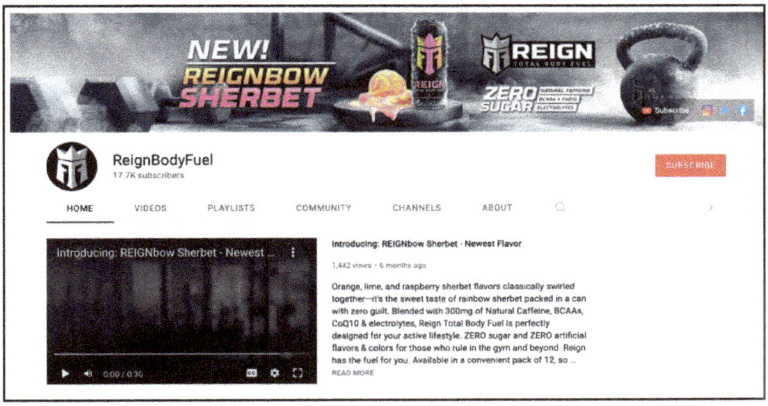
NEW!
REIGNBOW
SHERBET
REIGN
TOTAL BODY FUEL
ZERO
SUGAR
ReignBodyFuel
17.7K subscribers
SUBSCRIBE
HOME
VIDEOS
PLAYLISTS
COMMUNITY
CHANNELS
ABOUT
Introducing: REIGNbow Sherbet - Newest ...
0:00 / 0:30
Introducing: REIGNbow Sherbet - Newest Flavor
1,442 views • 6 months ago
Orange, lime, and raspberry sherbet flavors classically swirled together—it's the sweet taste of rainbow sherbet packed in a can with zero guilt. Blended with 300mg of Natural Caffeine, BCAAs, CoQ10 & electrolytes, Reign Total Body Fuel is perfectly designed for your active lifestyle. ZERO sugar and ZERO artificial flavors & colors for those who rule in the gym and beyond. Reign has the fuel for you. Available in a convenient pack of 12, so ...
READ MORE

xii

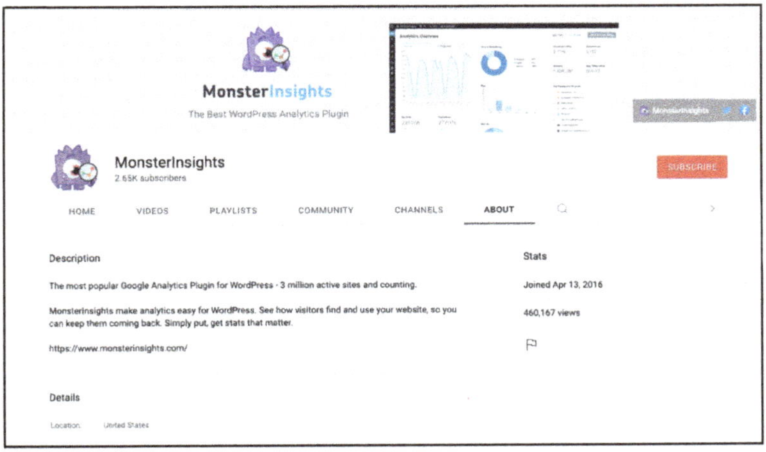
MonsterInsights
The Best WordPress Analytics Plugin
MonsterInsights
2.65K subscribers
SUBSCRIBE
HOME
VIDEOS
PLAYLISTS
COMMUNITY
CHANNELS
ABOUT
Description
The most popular Google Analytics Plugin for WordPress - 3 million active sites and counting.
MonsterInsights make analytics easy for WordPress. See how visitors find and use your website, so you can keep them coming back. Simply put, get stats that matter.
https://www.monsterinsights.com/
Details
Location: United States
Stats
Joined Apr 13, 2016
460,167 views

xiii

TikTok

TikTok is simple in terms of profile setup. Simply choose a username and profile photo in accordance with the henceforth established username/profile photo best practices and write a sub-80-character bio introducing your business. This must be short and snappy—there's no space even for an Instagram-style descriptor. Include emojis and note that keyword placement is completely irrelevant. Consider including a call-to-action in the form of a bio link (website, product/service page, or customized landing page is best) and tagline, such as "offer below" or "Instagram." Use a few down arrows as the last line of bio text. Finally, make sure to switch the profile from a personal account to a TikTok business account. This allows for analytics, an email contact button, and the website link implementation.

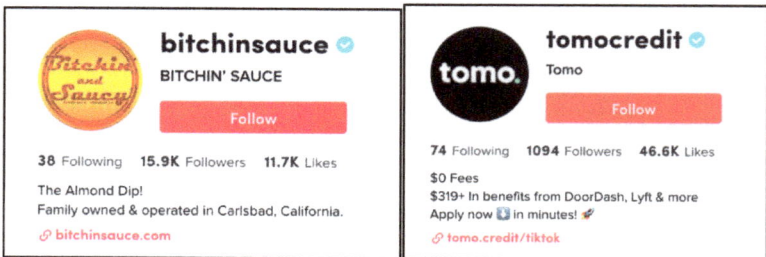

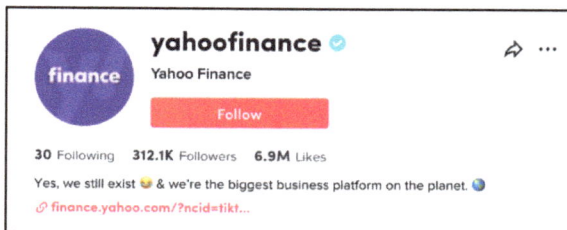

bitchinsauce ✓
BITCHIN' SAUCE
Follow
38 Following   15.9K Followers   11.7K Likes
The Almond Dip!
Family owned & operated in Carlsbad, California.
🔗 bitchinsauce.com

tomocredit ✓
Tomo
Follow
74 Following   1094 Followers   46.6K Likes
$0 Fees
$319+ In benefits from DoorDash, Lyft & more
Apply now 🔲 in minutes! 💸
🔗 tomo.credit/tiktok

yahoofinance ✓
Yahoo Finance
Follow
30 Following   312.1K Followers   6.9M Likes
Yes, we still exist 😌 & we're the biggest business platform on the planet. 🌐
🔗 finance.yahoo.com/?ncid=tikt...

Twitter

Establishing a presence on Twitter is similarly minimalistic; just choose a username and insert a profile photo, header graphic, location, bio, and website. Keep the bio short; interjected humor is common on the platform (note the second profile below).

xv

xvi

Twitter rounds out our look into establishing social profiles for your business. Upon completion of the prior steps, your business has a dynamic social presence covering all the major media platforms. Your business will begin to rank socially across all search engines and the social platforms you maintain a presence on.

This presents innate benefits: greater visibility leading to more customers. However, establishing a social presence is only the first step of a smart digital strategy—creating social content and advertisement on social media rounds out a strategy designed to allow and encourage scale far beyond that possible solely through the maintenance of a social presence. The next few portions of this book will focus on these imperatives: first on audience building (equivalent in concept to organic marketing), then on paid digital marketing, and finally on grassroots marketing strategies that leverage social networks in uncommon, but notably effective, ways.

5

Building an Audience

Establishing your digital presence is an impactful first step in ensuring exposure and winning more customers. However, there is only so much your profiles can do: to massively grow your business through digital means, two paths can be taken.

These two paths are audience-building and advertisement, which can essentially be thought of as "organic marketing" versus "paid marketing." While both require time and effort, they attack the problem of growing your business online from different angles. Organic marketing is all about creating great content that people engage with. If you can pull it off, it's low investment and has practically limitless scale.

Paid advertising is more stable and provides short-term returns, but rarely provides asymmetric or unexpected returns and, depending on how you choose to do it, usually requires more of an investment.

In this section, we'll examine audience-building as a path to growing your business online. I personally believe in this strategy more than advertising—it's a creative and fun endeavor (if done correctly), and one that I've seen completely change the game for many small businesses, including several of mine, in a low-cost manner.

Building an audience online is done on social media apps. Our definition of "social media" is liberal—email, for example, is a social medium, as well as text. Regardless of the specific app, audience-building requires content creation: by putting out content people enjoy, consume, and share into the world, consumers who would never have otherwise heard about your business will be driven toward your products and services. At a high level, refer to the four types of content you can create (page fifteen), and your social strategy should incorporate some or all of these types.

It is best to build an audience that converts to bottom-line revenue and other KPIs through the following platforms. Keep in mind that content can be shared across multiple platforms—for example, one blog post can be shared to your website, Facebook page, LinkedIn account, and email list, and then shared as a story on Instagram. We'll get into this process later:

- **Website:** building out an email list through your website and creating some sort of newsletter or blog is essential.
- **Instagram:** a requisite for audience-building and content creation.
- **Facebook:** likewise, a great place to connect with your community and share all types of content.
- **LinkedIn**: LinkedIn can be quite lucrative and an opportune platform on which to re-share written content from a blog or newsletter.
- **TikTok:** no, it's not just for the kids. TikTok is highly scalable and relatively easy to gain a following on through short-form videos.

So, we have the types of content you could be making to build an audience, and the platforms you could be posting it on. Before moving on to the exact strategies and processes imperative to content creation, think back to the platforms you identified as being most valuable to your business. That was half of the puzzle—you can now mesh that information with the types of content that are best for each platform.

Say your social strategy identified your website, Facebook, and LinkedIn as being the most important mediums on which your business will establish itself. The primary content types outlined for this collection of platforms are long-form text, such as a blog, as well as a few videos to introduce your business across the website and Facebook page. In this hypothetical, you now have a clear idea of how you will build your audience—by creating a few high-quality videos to post across all platforms to introduce customers to your brand and offerings, and then by regularly creating written content to share to your email list, website, Facebook profile, and LinkedIn profile.

This is the thought process you should walk through to establish a clear idea of how your business will build itself an online audience and customer base.

We'll now explore best practices for creating content and growing an audience on all the social platforms identified thus far. Feel free to read only about the platforms you will actually be utilizing, or anything beyond as per your interest and to aid in an understanding of the general social audience-building space.

Building & Optimizing a Website

We'll begin with an admittedly larger subject than audience building. We'll explore not only how to grow an audience and turn that audience into customers through email marketing and blogging, but how to set up a website in the first place, as well as best practices for website development and SEO (search engine optimization, which refers to how well your website ranks on browsers such as Chrome).

While you may opt to outsource website development if you don't have a site already, having some basic knowledge of the workings of your website goes a long way.

Building a no-code website consists of the domain, website builder, and hosting plan. The domain is the URL of your website, such as mybusiness.com or mybusiness.org. The website builder is the framework through which you can edit your website, like the settings of a computer. Hosting is the server where the website's data is stored.

Thankfully, the process to set up domain hosting and a website is fairly easy nowadays, as well as cheap.

Begin by going to GoDaddy at godaddy.com. Here, you can search for the domain you'd like for the website of your business. "Yourbusinessname.com" is the best bet. If it's a common name, you may need to opt for .co, .org, or something of the like. Once you've identified a domain that's available, you're ready to set up hosting.

In my experience, WordPress is the best "website builder" for small businesses. Nearly 70% of the internet runs on WordPress, and it allows for near-complete control over a website, as well as a wide range of add-on functionalities. Other popular website builders, like Squarespace, Wix, and Weebly, offer an extremely limited range of tools.[11]

To set up WordPress hosting, you have a few options—GoDaddy starts WordPress hosting plans at $6.99 per month (domain not included), while BlueHost (bluehost.com) offers a WordPress hosting plan for $2.99. GoDaddy has somewhat of a simpler interface, but otherwise, the two services are nearly identical.

Whichever service you decide to go with, make sure you buy the domain through that provider. You can bundle a domain and hosting plan at the below links or else purchase them individually (just make sure to choose the correct domain when setting up the hosting plan, and not purchase a new one).

godaddy.com/en-in/hosting/WordPress-hosting
bluehost.com/WordPress

On both services, make sure to enable SSL (secure sockets layer), which attaches the site lock that's viewable each time you visit a verified website (e.g., the lock in the below visual, which is Google's way of saying a website is safe).

🔒 google.com

Now that your domain and hosting plan is set up, you can start building your website in WordPress. Whether in GoDaddy or

---

[11] In return, they simplify the website setup process. However, WordPress allows for the incorporation of easy drag and drop builders as well (like Elementor). If you're looking for an ultra-simplistic option, go with Squarespace, Wix, or Weebly, just know it's generally not the best option in the long run.

Bluehost, go to the products menus and click "edit my site" or some variation of such.

You'll find yourself in the WordPress dashboard, which will look something along the lines of this:

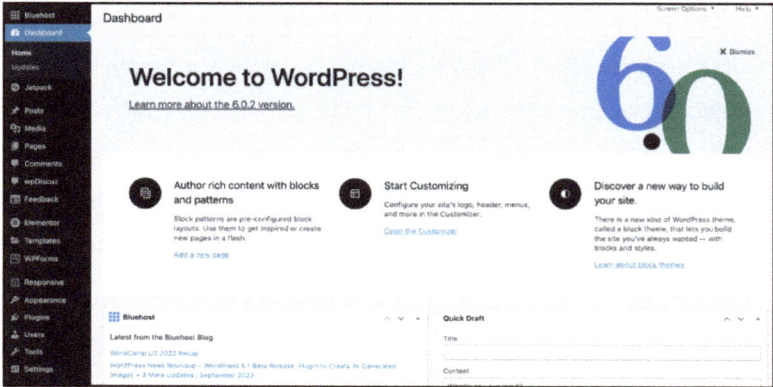

xvii

It can be a little intimidating at first glance, so let's break down the menu on the leftmost portion of the screen:

- **Posts** is where you can create and publish content.
- **Media** is where photos, videos, and documents are uploaded to the site.
- **Pages** is where you can manage the content (e.g., layout and words) of each part (for example, home page, about page, etc.) of the website.
- **Appearance** is where you can set the website theme, manage the structure, and customize the look.
- **Plugins** is where you can find an entire library of add-ons ready to add functionality to your site.

- **Users** lets you manage the people who have accounts on your site, ranging from admin to customers.
- **Settings** lets you manage some general facets and stylistic elements of your site.

Your website is currently unpublished. To get it ready for publication, begin by choosing a visual look for the website. Navigate to appearance > themes and pick a theme (simple is better to begin with) you feel represents your brand and business. You can also Google the best themes for your type of business to find alternatives that aren't on the built-in store.

Then, navigate to appearance > customize and set the site identity, global settings, footer, sidebar, and header to your liking. To create new pages on the website, edit all pages, or delete re-installed pages, click on pages > add new, pages > edit, or pages > trash. To change the top-level menu, which is what shows up on the website header, visit appearance > menus.

As you begin to fill in page content, such as on the home page and about page, note the "+" in the top-left corner of pages you're editing. This lets you insert page elements, called blocks, into the page. If you're not happy with the built-in WordPress page editor, consider installing the Elementor plugin, which offers slightly more advanced drag-and-drop editing.

Beyond Elementor, consider installing some of these essential plugins (all have a free plan):

SEO Plugin: Yoast SEO and Jetpack are two popular plugins that let you improve and better manage the search engine optimization of your website.

Analytics Plugin: MonsterInsights and Google Analytics are two popular plugins that provide advanced analytics.

Security Plugin: Akismet and Wordfence are two popular plugins that protect against spam and provide firewalls (also consider TrustedSite).

WPForms: create and add interactive forms to your website.

Updraft Plus: create automatic backups of your website.

WooCommerce: set up an online store to sell products.

SmashBalloon: add social media widgets.

OptinMonster: get more email subscribers.

HubSpot: utilize customer reputation management (CRM).

There are tens of thousands of plugins available, so consult the plugin library whenever you're looking to add functionality to your website.

You're now familiar with all the WordPress basics—how to pick a domain, set up hosting, add a theme, change the website's look, add and edit pages, change the navigation menu, and install plugins.

When it comes to stylistic and strategic website decisions, keep in mind that your website should reflect your brand identity in a visually appealing and straightforward manner. Don't go over the top with plugins or pages and limit plugin count to the essentials. Make sure to maximize search engine optimization (SEO) through the SEO plugin you've installed, as this will ensure that the website ranks over time (though it can take some time—to manually index your website on Google, which makes the process go faster, visit search.google.com/search-console). Additionally, if you're planning to sell products through your WordPress website, follow the WooCommerce setup process.

Once the website is up, note that to cultivate community and engage with potential customers, blogging and email marketing are the name of the game. Email marketing, especially, is a must-do for all businesses, while blogging is valuable in that it provides content that increases visibility on search and can be shared across other social platforms.

Email Marketing

Email is a massively pervasive form of social communication with nearly four billion worldwide addresses. 73% of polled consumers have said email is their preferred marketing channel, while the medium email marketing ROI is 122%.

Email marketing leverages email lists to sell products or services and strengthen customer relationships. It begins with capturing emails: namely, figuring out how to get your current and potential customers to give you their email addresses. This is most commonly achieved through email capture forms on landing and checkout pages—you've likely experienced this yourself when checking "sign up for our newsletter" boxes on checkout pages, or when entering your email into a website to receive a special discount or reward. Once you've established a funnel (acquisition strategy) to acquire emails, consider these classic email marketing strategies (we'll explore how to automate these email processes further on):

- **Greet new subscribers and customers with welcome emails** (and perhaps a reward). Immediately after a customer subscribes to the email list of your business, send them an email detailing a brief thank-you, company background, selling point, or reward. Aim to make this email feel personable, as the receiver has likely not had much prior interaction with your brand.

- **Regularly send a newsletter.** Newsletters are a powerful way to ensure customers stay in touch with your brand and business. Newsletters (most of which are sent out weekly) can feature news, customer and team stories, blog posts, and other social content.

- **Share business updates and product launches.** An email list is a perfect way to get news about new aspects of your business out to your customer base. Including some sort of discount or reward for early viewers is sure to increase engagement.

Thankfully, you don't have to do the work of sending out these emails yourself—rather, a variety of powerful automation services exist to make email marketing easy.

Mailchimp and Constant Contact: best overall.
Drip: best for e-commerce stores.

Hubspot: best CRM tool.

Sendinblue: best tools for growing a customer base.

Focus on automation when using these services. For example, set up a series of five emails to be sent to all new email subscribers over a period of five weeks (in addition to regular content), or a special thank you message or reward to be sent to customers that hit a certain spending milestone. Setting up automation of this type is not difficult: just explore tutorials on the email marketing platform you choose to work with.

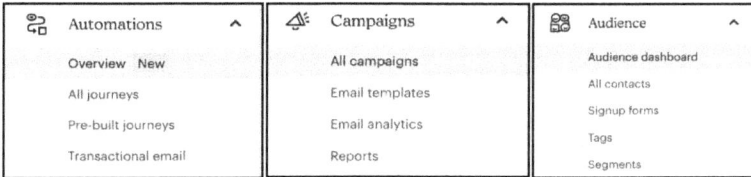

Automations ^	Campaigns ^	Audience ^
Overview New	All campaigns	Audience dashboard
All journeys	Email templates	All contacts
Pre-built journeys	Email analytics	Signup forms
Transactional email	Reports	Tags
		Segments

Automation, Campaign, and Audience tools from Mailchimp.com

Make sure to personalize all emails, A/B test headings and content to optimize open rates over time, and keep body text concise.

Let's now move on to blogging, which serves to further the depth and reach of email marketing if properly implemented.

Blogging

A blog is simply a website with chronologically ordered information, typically in an article-like format (long-form text).

Currently, nearly 600 million blogs exist on the internet, while 81% of businesses consider their blogs important (as per HubSpot) and small businesses that blog get 126% more lead growth than small businesses that do not blog (as per ThinkCreative).

Blogging serves to rank your website higher on Google and other search engines, meaning that more people discover your business. Blogging also lets you connect with your current audience and position your brand as an authority in your field.

You can easily set up a blog on your WordPress website by visiting the default "posts page" within the "pages" menu. This page will actually load a feed of your blog posts, which you can create within WordPress through "posts", "add new." You can download plugins such as Elementor, SeedProd, and Blog Designer to further customize the feel of your blog page.

When creating blog posts, focus on education-type content detailing a subject within your field of business. Posts should be at least a thousand words, though the ideal length for SEO (search engine optimization) is around 2,000-2,500 words. Additionally, ensure posts maximize their SEO through your choice of the SEO plugins described previously.

You should post an article on your blog at least once per week. This type of work is easily outsourced—we will examine the process of doing so throughout chapter seven. Blog posts can be shared in a newsletter (thus serving to drive email engagement) and across social accounts on other platforms.

Take note of some brands that successfully use blogs to expand their reach and further customer engagement:

xviii

xix

xx

Since blog posts will be an introduction of your brand and
business to many, ensure that messaging is consistent with the
grander brand identity and product offerings.

Growing on Instagram

Instagram is the old dog of social networks. It's the most established of the group other than Facebook and dominates in favorability versus Facebook among younger demographics. While Instagram has been incorporating new features in the past few years that explore the trends initialized by young apps such as TikTok (most notably "reels") the main function of the app is still as a means of sharing photo content.

Yes, growing on Instagram just through sharing photos has become exceedingly difficult over the years as algorithm changes hurt the chances of organic content performing well.

Instagram reels copy TikTok by presenting a short-form video feed to viewers. Reels provide the easiest way to get organic exposure. Any videos posted to TikTok should also be posted to reels (and YouTube shorts, as we'll get to later), and I've found that the supermajority of growth on my Instagram accounts now come from reels as opposed to organic reach on photos.

When growing an audience and creating content for Instagram, first consider differentiation. There are millions upon millions of accounts on Instagram in every niche, including that of your business. If it exists, someone is probably already posting about it on Instagram in some shape or form. The flip side of this is that differentiation is attractive—when people see new or unique things, they'll stick to it. Think about how you can differentiate within the niche of your business. Additionally, use color profiles to maintain a standard sense of style across all photos. This in and of itself allows for differentiation.

For those looking for a legitimate and effective way to speed run growth and reach real people, or even to add just a little boost to an account and content, Instagram ads and post promotions are a great solution. Of course, they do require some amount of money to begin, but if you're willing to spend that amount, growing a personal or business brand rapidly is not extraordinarily difficult.

Simply connect a Facebook account to your Instagram account and promote the content on your profile that you feel represents your brand the best. Set the budget and duration and start the promotion. Focus your overall campaign on a few high-converting posts (which you can identify through post analytics) if you're looking purely to gain followers, while if you want your like counts to increase across the board in addition to followers, split your overall budget across each new post, or at least across a multitude of posts. If you have the budget, I recommend incorporating promotions into your growth strategy early on—it's a

---

[12] @mentality and @frank_bod

great way to hit 10k followers fast, for example, but not so great once you're at 100k.

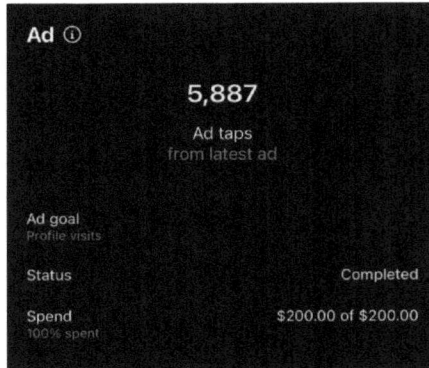

This $200 post promotion generated nearly 6,000 profile visits.

To this note, organic content must overwhelm growth derived from ads in the long term unless ads are unusually profitable. Ads of this nature are simply a complementary measure to support organic content and jump through some algorithmic and social construct loopholes (in terms of follower counts).

Next, note that Instagram automation consists of software that automatically likes posts, views videos, comments, and follows other accounts from your profile. The idea is that a person on the receiving end of a like, view, or comment may decide to check out your account and give it a follow. Such a result may only occur once per 500 engagements, but if those actions can be performed by a bot 10,000 times per day, follower accounts can grow quickly (at least initially). Automation services do cost some amount of money, ranging from 20 or fewer dollars per month to several hundred. They hold practically no value in the long run, as growth from organic content is always king, but they can be useful when starting out from zero.

Instagram tips and tricks:

- The easiest video length to get views, in my experience, is less than 20 seconds. Beyond 30s gets more difficult, though this depends upon your niche.

- The first 3 seconds matter (bait) and the last 3 seconds matter just as much or more (hook). If you have great bait, people will watch until the hook, and if the hook is great, they'll rewatch. You need both elements to hit >100% watch time, which is where you can start to pull real views.

- Visually appealing and high energy works best unless a lack of high energy provides comedic effect.

- Frequency doesn't matter if videos are good enough (quality beats all, one viral video is better than fifty flops), but posting at least once per day is ideal for starting up an account. Again, however, if videos are good enough, a minimum volume doesn't exist.

- Simplifying and automating the production pipeline is key. Creating challenges that require you to post daily is an easy way to do this and remove creative effort from the equation.

- When it comes to Instagram reels, posting must be consistent to level up in the bucket algorithm. Stopping for a few weeks dropped me from 50-100k average views to barely breaking 10k for several more weeks.

- Like and comment ratios do not matter when it comes to reels, as evidenced by these videos (watch time is key for all short-form video, not like/comment ratios):

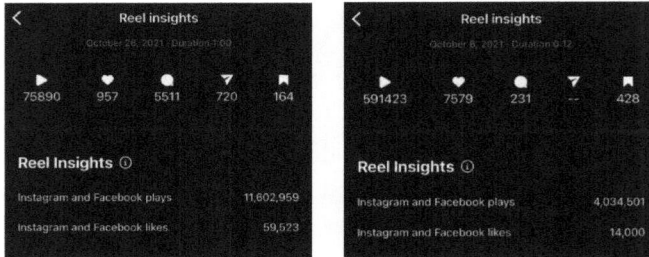

In sum, Instagram presents a wide range of powerful content options and a massive audience to back it up. Every business can find its home on the platform and leverage the tools available in the pursuit of a stronger community and bottom line.

Growing on TikTok

Even by the standards of social media, TikTok is crazy. The ByteDance-launched app hit 2.6 billion installations within 5 years of launch, largely due to its capitalization on short-form content, which other platforms (most notably Instagram through reels and YouTube through shorts) have quickly moved to copy. TikTok was unique because of its bucket-based algorithm, which "tests" content before promoting it to larger audiences. This serves the purpose of allowing nearly any video to organically go viral, assuming engagement is good enough from the get-go. This drastically contrasts with the algorithms of apps such as Instagram and YouTube, on which starting from scratch is notoriously difficult.

The downside of an extremely opportunistic algorithm and a short-from content platform is that views matter less (say, 100k views on TikTok is not as valuable as 100k views on YouTube) and emigrating a following to other platforms is extremely difficult (say, out of 100k TikTok followers, just 1k may convert to Instagram followers). So, while it may be much easier to hit ten thousand followers from scratch on TikTok, those ten thousand followers don't mean nearly as much in terms of true fans nor as a means of monetization versus ten thousand followers on Instagram, YouTube, or Facebook.

My own experiences exemplify these ideas. The first video I ever posted on TikTok got more views than the previous two years I'd spent on Instagram and YouTube combined. I was able to 6x the size of my overall personal social media following in one year on TikTok, and yet the rewards were dismal off-platform: barely any crossover and no money earned at all for 40+ million direct views over three accounts, as well as double that in reposts. With this in mind, TikTok is great as a top-of-the-funnel and social proof tool, while TikTok ads represent a direct opportunity within the platform to grow a small business.

Following years of slow growth, I was able to quickly expand my exposure and view counts through TikTok.

I'll impart the video format I used to fast-track growth, as well as general best practices for growing a business through TikTok.

Success on TikTok begins with the approach. TikTok is all about providing value—you're competing for the time of viewers, and the videos and associated accounts that consistently provide the most value capture the most time from viewers, which gets those videos promoted to wider audiences, thus encouraging viral, snowball-like cycles for content creators. Within the niche of your business, ensuring long-term success is a matter of identifying the value your videos provide and the value your audience wants, optimizing future videos based on such insights, and repeating. If something hits, run with it and build upon it. If it doesn't, take notes.

The TikTok algorithm is bucket-based. Bucket-based algorithms give everyone the chance to go viral, as opposed to basing reach largely on audience size. The bucket algorithm works as follows, though on a much more abstract level (e.g., "buckets" are not literally separated by an order of magnitude):

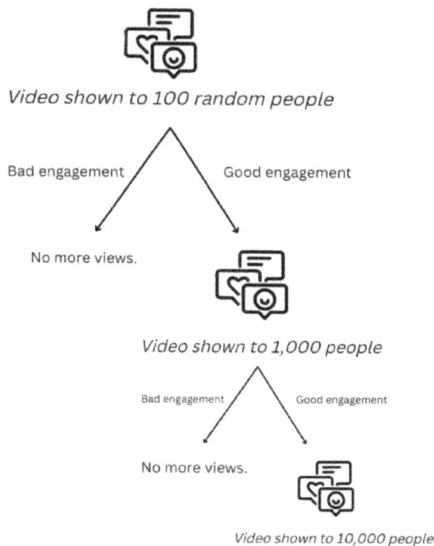

Video shown to 100 random people

Bad engagement   Good engagement

No more views.

Video shown to 1,000 people

Bad engagement   Good engagement

No more views.

Video shown to 10,000 people

Each video is shown to a certain number of people. Depending on how those people engage with the given video, it may or may not progress to the next bucket, in which the video is shown to a substantially greater number of people.[13] Minus the odd case, this progresses until the video reaches some maximum number of views

---

[13] How long they watch it, how much they like, share, and comment on it.

within its bucket, at which point it levels off. Some videos may take days to start gaining momentum, and others may trail off in a day or two, versus as in the case of a viral video, weeks. As your audience grows larger and you post more videos, your account levels up in the algorithm, and your videos are guaranteed to fall into a higher bucket. This is why large creators get millions of views no matter what they post: in a sense, they're able to skip the grading process.[14] When posting videos, you'll notice that they will often gain a substantial number of views quickly, then stop gaining, then start again at a further date. Sometimes, the interval between the high-growth periods is only minutes or hours, while sometimes that difference can be days or even weeks in length. As the buckets get bigger, the time taken to fill up the bucket expands, meaning that a video bucketed up from a few hundred to a few thousand views may reach that in just a few hours, while a video moving from half a million to five million views may stretch that growth more evenly over days or weeks. So, what does this mean for your TikTok account and strategy?

First, note that pulling more views does get easier as you get bigger since the TikTok algorithm largely guarantees all videos on an account a certain place in the tier-based system. This is neither a hard rule nor one that should be focused upon. Rather, keep trying to make the best videos you can, and eventually mix the bread and butter of the account into videos that audiences will still engage with (since, at such a point, you've developed a brand to the extent that people will watch regardless) but require much less effort than the

---

[14] Rightfully so, since they've proved themselves in the past from an algorithmic sense

main growth drivers. Still, as the adage goes, keep the main thing the main thing, and remember that producing great videos initially, and lots of them, is necessary to ensure a quick rise in the bucket algorithm.

A second way these concepts impact your TikTok account and video strategy is that small improvement in video analytics, primarily average watch time and watched-full-video percentage, yield massive results, and vice versa. This isn't just rhetoric, or some moral standard—optimization matters, and to illustrate this point are analytics from two real videos on an account of mine:

476k views

10.5/11s AWT (average watch time)

54.5% WFV (watched full video)

Video performance			
Total time watched	Average time watched	Watched full video	Reached Audience
1437h:27m:13s	10.6s	54.5%	439.3K

5.2m views

11.9/11s AWT

56.3% WFV

Video performance			
Total time watched	Average time watched	Watched full video	Reached Audience
17353h:18m:25s	11.9s	56.3%	4.6M

The second video got 10x as much exposure off a 5-10% difference in engagement. Situations like this are present everywhere—while over time all videos on an account are algorithmically likely to hit a certain minimum view count, achieving success beyond that standard and virality on a regular basis is all about the bottom line: small improvements, compounded, yielding massive results.

The takeaways here should be that the conscious pursuit of optimization and iteration is necessary to ensure growth, and once a viral format is found, it should be wrung for all its worth. Really, the heart of the matter, and the core concept in relation to the above, is value and one's ability to adapt content to meet an audience's wants over time.

Success on TikTok, as well as on all social content platforms, comes down to the question of why someone watches a video. I view it as coming down to the E&E rule: entertainment versus education. All media content exists on two spectrums, one of entertainment value, and one of educational value. Identifying the value your videos provide is identifying where on the E&E spectrum a video and niche exist and then asking this question: does it provide enough E&E relative to the best content in the world in your niche, or relative to your business competitors? If not—if your videos do not provide as much or more education, entertainment, or some combination of the two then the best videos in the world in your niche, holistic and breakthrough success is unlikely.

Thankfully, there is a way around this—I've essentially stated that success on social media is extremely difficult if you're not the best at something. Alternatively, you may simply create your own niche—that way, providing either the most entertainment value or the most educational value in the world in that niche is much easier, because you're literally the only one doing it in that way. Essentially, you're lowering the bar, and mixing in the value of surprise. So, while success is certainly made possible by beating the competition, sustainable success is most easily achieved by creating content that has no competition.

Take the niche I built my personal brand and business in—there are millions of fitness creators on social media, most of whom were more knowledgeable, stronger, better looking, or better at video production than I was. As opposed to trying to compete against them, I simply chose to do something in the fitness niche that no one else was doing in the way I was doing it. That thing was fitness challenges—it turned out that the first time I did a challenge, I pulled in several million views and tens of thousands of followers in just a month. By creating a new niche as opposed to competing in an old one, I became instantly unique, offered shock value, and beat out people who, on paper, were superior social media producers to me in every way.

All said, I'd like to get into some specific best practices that I've learned over the past few years on TikTok:

- Like ratios are largely irrelevant.
- Share and comment ratios are largely irrelevant.
- Hashtags are mostly irrelevant, more so if you have an audience. Note that TikTok practically does hashtags for you once they've figured out your audiences, so hashtags really aren't that necessary. Just use 2-3 per video when you're starting out, and you wean off them once you have at least 10k followers, an established niche, and solid view counts.

A case study from a business Instagram page of mine with no prior established audience (800 or so followers):

11.5m views, 59.3k likes.
4.0m views, 235 comments.

The like and comment ratios on this video were incredibly poor—still, just based on watch time, the videos were able to perform well. I'll say it again: watch time is the end-all metric to prioritize. Next, note the general TikTok metrics to aim for:

- Watched full video (WFV): - 50% in general, 60-70% if shorter.
- Average watch time (AWT): - >100% if under 15 seconds, >125% if under 10 seconds. Minimum - 75%

These numbers, in my experience, perform within a range of a few hundred thousand views up to a few million views, as follows:

Length: 6 seconds

Video performance			
Total time watched	Average time watched	Watched full video	Reached Audience
2311h:53m:31s	9.0s	69%	842.6K
+1.2% (+0.01%)	+0.0s (+0%)	0% (-0.01%)	+7 (+0.01%)

Length: 9 seconds

Video performance			
Total time watched	Average time watched	Watched full video	Reached Audience
12178h:41m:0s	12.1s	69.5%	3.3M
+1.8m (+0.01%)	+0.0s (+0%)	0% (-0.01%)	+8 (+0.01%)

Length: 17 seconds

Video performance			
Total time watched	Average time watched	Watched full video	Reached Audience
18583h:12m:12s	16.0s	59.3%	3.9M
+27.8m (+0.01%)	+0.0s (+0%)	0% (-0.01%)	+170 (+0.01%)

Growing on Facebook

As the quintessential social media platform popular among older demographics, not to mention one focused on community, developing a presence on Facebook is a must-do to reach not only customers in your community but as many of Facebook's 2.9 billion users as possible.

As per the social presence section, you should currently have a filled-out Facebook business profile.

Beyond an optimized profile, building an audience on Facebook boils down to creating and sharing content, engaging with your audience, and running ads. Ads are not a requirement in growing a page, but Facebook has been moving its algorithms away from promoting organic content in recent years, as the average organic reach of a Facebook post is now around 5% of the page's total likes (meaning very few followers organically see the content you post).

Right when you start your page, leverage your existing community and connections to build an initial audience. For example, if you have a physical location, ask regular customers to follow you on Facebook, or ask the same of friends. A starting circle of engaged customers and friends can go a long way in terms of organic reach.

Then, focus on establishing a strong content pipeline. You should post at least once per day (aim for this, but remember that quality wins over quantity) and a maximum of twice per day. Overall, content should be some mix of business updates, relevant tips and suggestions, partner, customer, or community profiles, interests, re-shared content, and whatever else is relevant to the business or target audience (ideally, it's both relevant to the business and engaging to the target audience). This content should be some mix of photos, videos, and text—multi-media posts, such as an article with a header image and walkthrough video, usually performs best versus any single media type. Follow best practices for content creation, such as strong titles, engaging visuals, and targeted (no more than three) hashtags. Use analytics over time to adjust the times you should post to maximize engagement.

We'll explore influencer marketing further on—keep this in mind as an immensely valuable tool when it comes to building an audience on Facebook as well as every other social platform.

If you're a business with a physical location, focus on creating content tiered around your local community. Join and create community groups to engage with customers around a specific subject (for example, a group could be created for each physical location, an annual event, or a business vertical). Hosting local events and advertising your Facebook page throughout is a great way to build a local audience, as well as direct advertising to your local community through Facebook ads.

If your business doesn't have a dedicated physical location or operates purely online, follow this same ethos—create and join groups to engage with your target audience, and follow it up with regular content that appeals to the target audience.

For either type of business, make sure to use the link post feature, where you can paste a URL into the create post box and Facebook will share a preview of the link. Also use Facebook stories, just like you would Instagram stories, as a means to regularly engage with your following without having to share a high-effort post. Regularly pin top-performing or highly relevant posts to the top of your Facebook page and encourage employees or friends to re-share content.

Make sure to engage with your audience across your content as well as theirs, and regularly offer opportunities to engage with your brand, offer feedback and suggestions, and receive discounts, rewards, or recognition.

Let's look at some small businesses that are effectively growing an audience and customer base on Facebook:

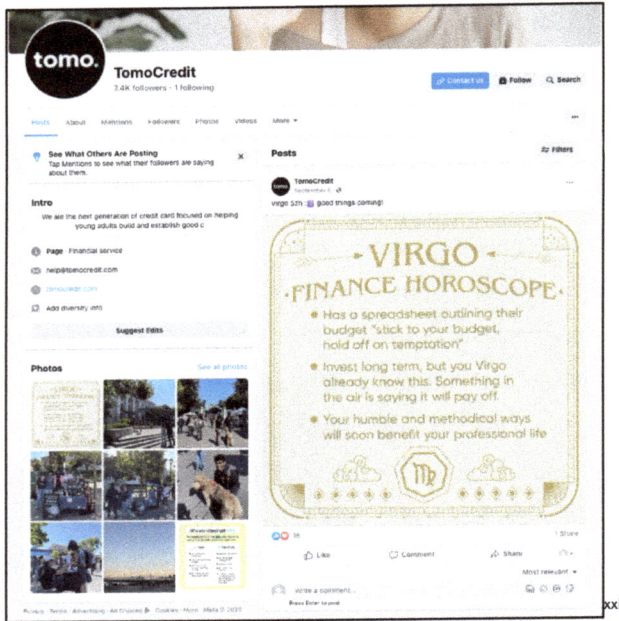

Note the engaging content and multitude of shared photos.

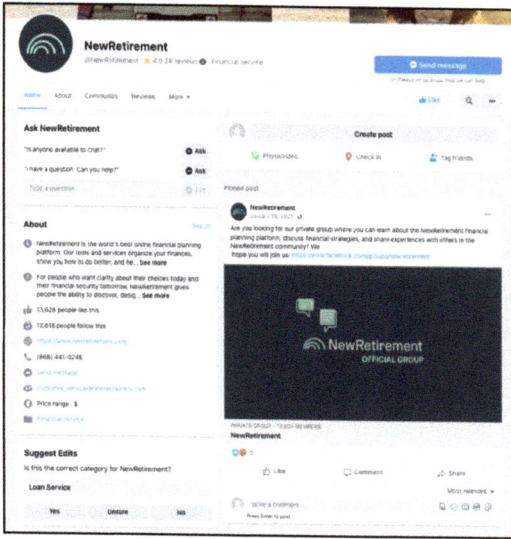

Note how @NewRetirement lets users directly ask questions over Messager and pinned a relevant call-to-action post.

Growing on YouTube

YouTube is different from the platforms explored prior in that it's solely focused on a different medium: long-form video. Video is a different beast to tackle than other forms of content as there's simply no way to get around the work of it; at the end of the day, no one can fake a good video about their business.[15] The same cannot be said about Tweets, articles, or website design.

So, YouTube is difficult for these reasons, but the spoils are immense—2 billion unique people use the website each month (second only to Google.com), 80% of U.S marketers are confident YouTube videos convert well, and 70% of YouTube viewers say they've purchased a product after learning about it in a YouTube ad. That's just for products purchased through ads—for businesses and creators with successful YouTube channels, engaged fans quickly turn into loyal and long-term customers. In fact, people retain 95% of a message consumed via video versus 10% when reading it in text, and this phenomenon directly translates into brand retention and impact.

So, while it is initially more difficult for businesses to build a following on YouTube relative to most other social platforms, the spoils of success on a per-follower basis outstrip other platforms.

Most businesses that create content on YouTube position themselves as authorities in their spaces by creating educational content. Many also post videos detailing how to use their platform,

---

[15] Content detailing the physical aspect of your business, at least, requires a certain degree of effort. A surprising volume of YouTube content as a whole is, in fact, outsourced.

interviews with founders and team members, industry news, and event coverage.

Note these businesses, all of which are effectively creating content that drives viewers towards their products and services:

xxii

xxiii

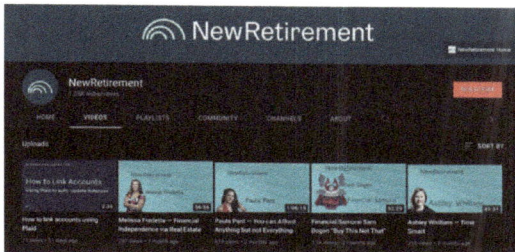
xxiv

Note the use of YouTube shorts by Manscaped, the strong banner by NerdWallet, and the long-form content by NewRetirement.

So, when going about YouTube for your business, think about the type of content you want to create within your niche: is there a gap in knowledge faced by your customers? What's the asymmetric knowledge present in you, your team, and your business that lets you do what you do, and how can you package that for an audience on YouTube? These questions will define your identity and content strategy on YouTube.

I've always found it helpful to immediately write out a bunch of ideas for videos right after coming up with a channel concept. Initially focus on videos with strong hooks (so they'll perform well as YouTube ads) or videos that you know will resonate well within your community or professional circle.

While on the subject, YouTube ads can be a powerful and cost-effective tool for increasing exposure and growing a channel early on. The average cost per view (CPV) on YouTube ads is just $0.026 (though I've gotten this under $0.01). This means, essentially, that you could be paying 1 cent for a real person to watch at least 30 seconds of your video. This equates to $10 for 1,000 views and $1,000 for 100,000 views. Off the bat, putting just a few hundred dollars into ad spend of this type can do wonders for a new channel.

In sum, growing on YouTube is all about putting out videos that people watch. These elements determine how watchable videos are, and thus how well they end up performing:

Quality: proper lighting, quality audio and sound design, punchy editing, and clean shot structures aren't everything, but they sure do help. Though dependent upon the type of video, a good camera, mic set, and place to film (sometimes a green screen makes things easier, or perhaps you'll opt for graphics-only content with voiceovers) is usually required.

Intro: on average, nearly a quarter of viewers, leave a video within its first ten seconds. So, focus on making sticky intros.

Length: people don't want enormously long videos: the average length of a video on the YouTube homepage is right around 14 minutes. It's nearly always better to err on the side of brevity given an interest in maximizing watch time. Aim for viewer retention (APV) of 50% or higher, as evidenced by the disparity in the APCs and resulting view counts of the below videos.

Average percentage viewed	Views	Impressions	Impressions click-through rate
47.3%	14,686	213,790	4.5%

Average percentage viewed	Views	Impressions	Impressions click-through rate
57.0%	5,684,773 496.0K – 803.0K	116,094,388	3.8%

Average percentage viewed	Views	Impressions	Impressions click-through rate
54.7%	6,731,966 531.0K – 1.1M	127,743,848	4.1%

xxv

Title and Thumbnail: your thumbnails are how you introduce yourself, and first impressions last. Thumbnail design aims to present the video concept (without lying) in the most intriguing, I-must-click-you light possible.

Like thumbnails, titles are one of the first ways in which a potential viewer will interact with your videos. Titles circle back to the purpose of the video: what's the overarching theme of the content you're creating, and who are you trying to reach? If you're trying to reach a GenZ audience with an entertainment-focused video, for example, titles should use shared lingo and feel informal. Yet, if you're creating advanced tutorials for an adult audience, you may opt for a more straight-to-the-point or structured title. In this manner, always seek to curate the title to the video, and make sure the messaging of titles and thumbnails match.

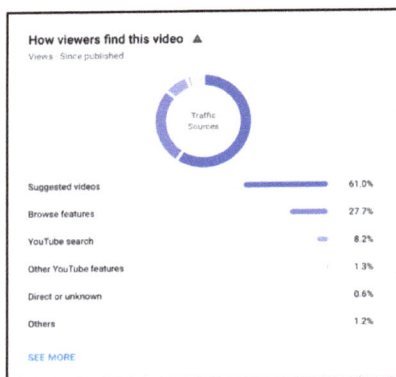

The importance of thumbnails is evidenced by the previous image, as a supermajority of views are derived from suggested videos and browse features, each of which displays videos only through their thumbnail and title.

Within a title, think about incorporating a hook, keywords, and numbers, creating urgency, clearly defining the solution or value

being provided, and using emotive words. Take note of these
elements throughout the following titles:

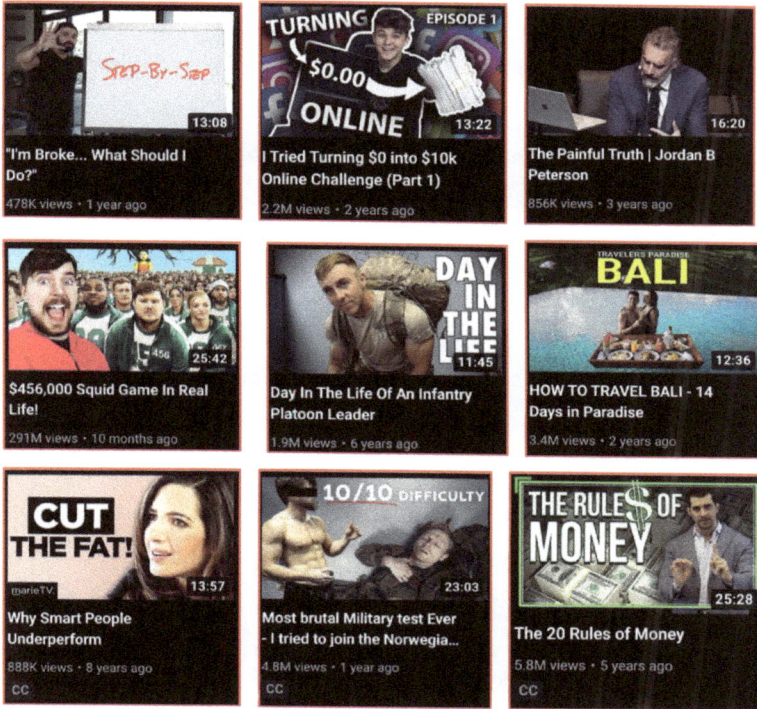

xxvi

1. The title asks a question that appeals to a substantial
   portion of people while the thumbnail further reinforces the
   concept and structure of the video.
2. The title appeals to everyone through a common incentive.
   Multiple parts infer depth.
3. An intriguing question is backed by a thumbnail alluding to
   the professional nature of the speaker and, therefore, video.

4. The video concept is based on a then-current trend, while the dollar value infers that the concept is pulled off (e.g., not just clickbait).

5. The clear title presents novelty, while the simplistic thumbnail reinforces the concept.

6. The value proposition is very clear, a number is incorporated, and the thumbnail is visually stunning.

7. The title text hooks people who regard themselves as smart (the target audience of the creator) and intrigue is increased through the text in the thumbnail.

8. Relevant keywords are placed in the back half of the title, while the first half (and the thumbnail) alludes to novelty.

9. Social proof is inferred through the suit and well-designed thumbnail.

Keywords: Use around ten semi-specific keywords in the "tags" section of each video. Note that YouTube states "tags play a minimal role in helping viewers find your video"—still, especially when just starting out, these keywords help the algorithm group and rank content. In the below image, keep in mind the specificity of keywords relative to the subject of the video (that being a 2000-squat challenge).

Value! All the elements described prior are important. Ultimately, each is about packaging videos in an optimal manner. What matters most of all is the video itself—as with all social content, the amount of time people stick around will inevitably correlate with the amount of value you provide to them, whether that's some form of education, entertainment, or both (no matter how great the thumbnail, title, or intro is). In sum, always lead with the viewer's wants and needs. If you provide value, you'll win.

Thus far, we've explored content ideation and how to make a great video. Let's now consider methods and strategies to maximize growth (beyond ads and influencer marketing, as covered further on):

Frequency: once a week is a solid minimum. Quality, however, should always trump quantity.

Community: promote your channel across other social platforms and throughout the pre-existing community and network of your business.

Clip: cut up your longer-form videos and share them as YouTube shorts, as well as across Instagram, TikTok, Facebook, and wherever else you have a presence in short-form video. Group videos by playlists on YouTube.

Engage & Reward: host giveaways or offer discounts. Post videos with other creators and businesses.

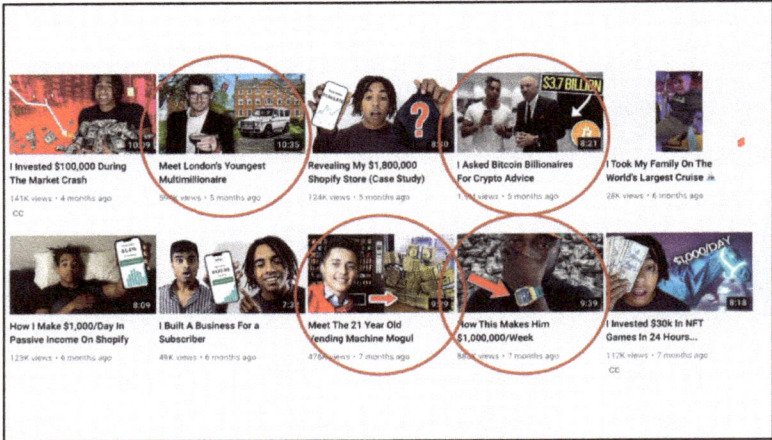

xxvii

Note how Jordan Welch regularly incorporates popular figures in his niche into his videos. This type of content consistently outperforms his other videos.

xxviii

Note how Beardbrand adds most of their videos to various playlists to increase search presence and encourage viewers to watch multiple videos in one sitting.

Monetization: Once your YouTube channels reach 1,000 subscribers and 4,000 hours of watch time, you can start earning money from ads placed by YouTube on the video. You can view these eligibility requirements under the monetization tab at studio.youtube.com.

Earnings from videos is based on RPM (revenue per thousand views). Niches earn different RPMs as per the amount of money advertisers within that niche are willing to pay. In this manner, finance videos earn higher RPMs than gaming videos since finance companies are willing to pay more to have their ads shown to YouTube viewers. In addition to earning revenue from ads placed on your videos once you're monetized, you can control how many ads are placed on a given video, as well as where each ad is placed. Generally, place one pre-roll ad and one mid-roll ad at around the eight-minute mark (depending upon the length of the video).[16]

You may choose to re-invest earnings from YouTube into video promotions. To exemplify this strategy, take the below video, which generated $5,800 in AdSense revenue (AdSense being Google's monetization platform, which handles ad revenue payouts).

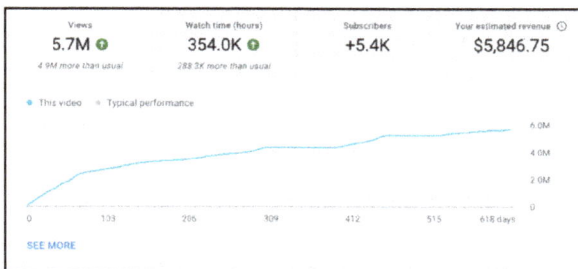

Views	Watch time (hours)	Subscribers	Your estimated revenue
5.7M	354.0K	+5.4K	$5,846.75
4.9M more than usual	288.3K more than usual		

SEE MORE

---

[16] Alternatively, place a second ad slightly before retention starts to drop off.

If the revenue derived from the previous visual was put back into ads at a CPV of $0.01 (as above), an additional 580,000 views could be directed toward an ad or video, thus earning several hundred more subscribers and an approximate $600 in additional revenue.

In this manner, businesses on YouTube can either reinvest earnings into video promotions through YouTube ads or use earnings to cover the cost of content creation. This speaks to the value of YouTube not only as a tool to drive customers further down a funnel, but to generate top-line revenue.

Once monetized, you can leverage the Teespring integration within YouTube to sell merchandise from a "shop" section directly under your YouTube videos. To explore this feature, visit "merchandise" under "monetization" in studio.youtube.com.

Above all, lead with the mindset of YouTube being a long-term game. Results quickly snowball, but it may take a quite a while to reach that first hundred, thousand, or ten thousand subscribers. Throughout the process, remember that consistency and value will win out—if you and your business do those two things, you'll be privy to the game-changing benefits of a successful YouTube presence.

Growing on Twitter

Twitter is a platform of quick interactions and fast-paced culture. Brands that do well on Twitter have their thumb on the cultural pulse not only of their field, but of society. Witty or insightful commentary on trends and news, engaging or controversial content relating to your branding and business, and satire typically perform the best. In all these cases, do your best to create content that people will retweet and add commentary to. This, ultimately, is how viral tweets and threads (threads are strings of interrelated tweets, perhaps to explore an idea that can't be explained in a single tweet, created by responding to one's own tweets) blow up.

If anything, do not appear overly edited or professional as a brand on Twitter. Twitter is all about community and culture, and the best way to win the hearts (and the wallets) of users is through creative and engaging content, not by pitching your business or products (unless they happen to be really engaging or unique enough on their own). People can see right through anyone who's not "in the know" and bringing in help to add relevance if you aren't a Twitter user yourself is a far superior strategy.

Next, don't make your brand seem off-limits—engage through comments, build relationships with customers, encourage retweets, and follow (some) people back.

Post at least 1-2 times a day on your Twitter account. This should vary as per current events that your business can reasonably add commentary to. Retweet at bare minimum several times per week. Note that engagement is usually the highest between 9-10 am (as always, adjust timing as per your Twitter analytics over time).

Check out some historical great brand tweet

@netflix indirectly advertises the show (the name of which is subtly placed on the bottom left of the image) through a witty line.

@Xbox leverages engaging content to show a personable side of the Xbox team.

Note the use of threads and the incentive @SlimJim created for viewers to engage with the post.

Growing on LinkedIn

Audience-building on LinkedIn begins with profile-building. Ensure that your personal LinkedIn page, as well as that of your business, is completely filled out. Profiles with complete information get on average 30% more views, while this differential expands for profiles regularly posting content. Make sure to fill out some showcase pages, which are affiliated extensions of your company's page used to highlight a business unit, initiative, or vertical. Finally, ensure that all profile elements of every page are set to public.

As always, first draw in an audience from outside sources. Ensure that you have maximized the connections of your personal LinkedIn page and that employees follow your LinkedIn business page. Finally, make sure to join and participate in relevant LinkedIn groups.

Beyond these SEO and optimization basics, increasing exposure and building an audience for your business on LinkedIn requires content creation. LinkedIn offers easy content creation tools through the business page super admin view and lets page admins create and add content through a wide variety of tools, notably including polls and an entire article-building sandbox.

As per the digital strategy you've created, it's most efficient to simply re-share content on LinkedIn that was initially designed for other platforms, and vice versa. For example, if your business already has a blog, just take that content, alter it to fit into your LinkedIn page, and share it to your LinkedIn profile.

Posts featuring a mix of content types, such as a header image, blog post, or poll perform the best. Make sure to incorporate a variety of relevant hashtags into content and break up longer posts into short paragraphs and headers.

Share at least 1-2 posts a week. Beyond posting on your business page, regularly post on your personal profile to drive potential leads toward your business, and regularly engage on both profiles in comment sections. Make it easy for employees to post LinkedIn content, such as during company events, promotions, milestones, etc.

As you grow, keep up with analytics to measure what visitors are or aren't engaging with, as well as what demographics constitute those visitors. Aggregate this information to make decisions on content ideation and strategy in the future.

If your brand works with influencers or other businesses, tag them in posts, and encourage them (better yet, coordinate with them) to tag your brand in return.

Finally, consider using LinkedIn ads to speedrun growth. This process is outlined in the advertising section.

These strategies ensure a holistic means of not just gaining a following and consumer base on LinkedIn, but ensuring that your business remains visible, generates leads in a professional environment, and maximizes business opportunities.

Note some examples of well-done small business LinkedIn profiles on the next page.

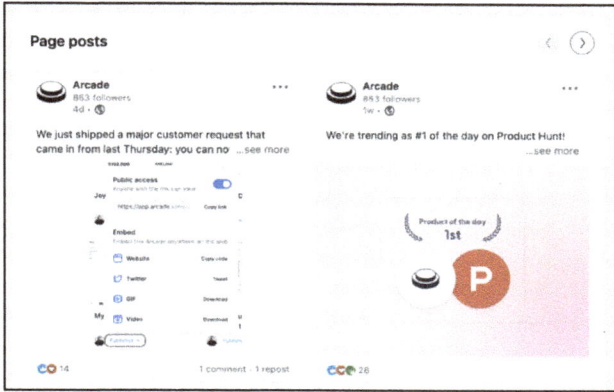

xxix

Note the mix of company updates and engaging longer-form content.

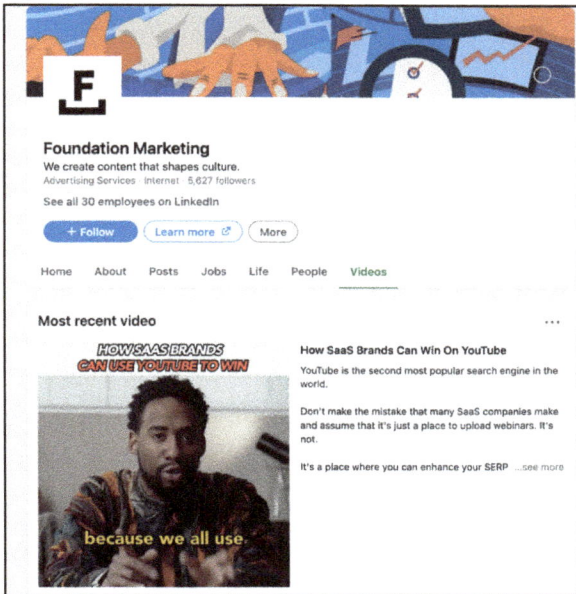

xxx

Note the use of quality video content to convey brand authority and drive engagement.

Growing on Pinterest

Pinterest is all about visuals. Growing on Pinterest starts with a consistent stream of quality images—if this pipeline isn't already incorporated into your business (such as in the case of a fashion or real estate company), putting effort into building a Pinterest audience is not the right move.

Pinterest is based on boards, which represent a central theme under which images are organized. Images from the internet can be "pinned" to a board, or images already on Pinterest can be "re-pinned" into another board. Pins can be commented upon.

So, growing on Pinterest reflects the number of images you put out, the number of boards you have, and the number of pins and re-pins you orchestrate. A minimum of five pins per day (preferably a few dozen) are required to grow an audience. Mashable and Pinerily found that Saturdays, afternoons, and evenings are the best days and times engagement-wise.

As for the content itself, Pinterest is designed around high-quality images with no human faces (figures/bodies are fine), no text or borders, and engaging visual content. For each pin and board, make sure to fill out the associated descriptions with keyword-rich content that includes your brand name. Visit trends.pinterest.com for content ideas. Finally, note that videos can be posted, so reposting short-form content is a great way to recycle successful content. Just make sure it's relevant to your Pinterest audience.

Regularly posting pins from a variety of websites (primarily, of course, your own) is best accompanied by regular engagement through group boards, comment sections, and content posted by other brands.

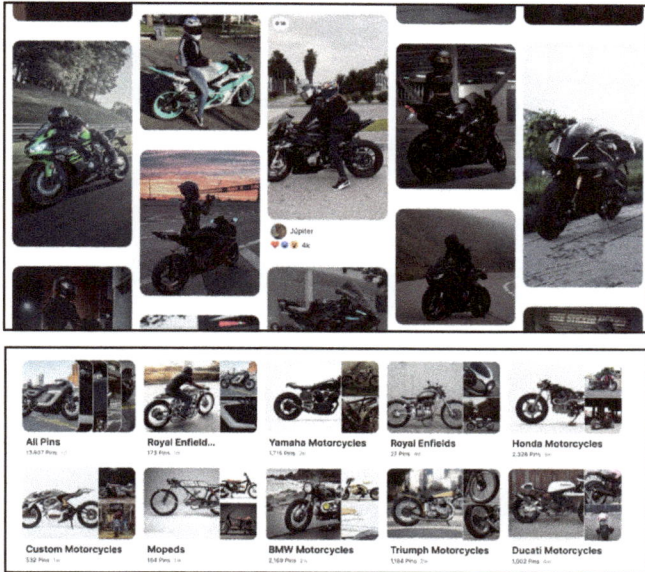

Note the consistent feel of Pinterest content, as well as the pure volume of pins on each board.

I'll say it again: Pinterest is a must-do for visual brands, especially for those selling products or services online. If that's you, at least re-share the photos you're already using within your business to the platform. Growth will snowball over time as users find and re-pin your content.

6

Creating Social Content

I n this section, we'll briefly cover some basics of video, photo, and graphics-based content creation.

Graphics

Most businesses operating on social media heavily incorporate graphic design into their content strategy. This genre of posts is usually visually simple and colorful. It transmits information through text and simple vector designs (e.g., simplistic images, cartoons, or traced shapes).

Graphics of this kind are not extraordinarily difficult to make and just require some basic knowledge in using any number of online design tools. You can outsource this kind of work, which is usually cheap (outsourcing is covered in the upcoming automation and sustainability chapter) or do it yourself. The latter is usually done on the following platforms:

Canva: Canva is an ultra-simplistic, do-it-yourself graphic design tool. It's free and offers a variety of pre-built templates.

Photoshop: Photoshop presents a complete suite of photo-editing tools. It requires a bit more time to learn versus an option like Canva and costs $20 per month (depending upon your choice of Creative Cloud plan), but presents a professional, end-all editing environment.

Photopea: Photopea is a free service modeled after Photoshop. It represents a mix between the two services described prior.

To get inspiration for the copyrighting and style of the graphics put out by your business, it's best to look at what competitors or brands you're looking to emulate are doing and work back from there. Focus on simple messages and text (not the time for paragraphs nor thorough explanations!) and incorporate brand strategy and identity.

Photo

xxxii

Photographic content is the intermediate level in terms of the difficulty between graphics and video. Good photos don't require obscenely expensive cameras; most relatively cheap ($1-2 thousand) Canon cameras are more than enough (rented gear also gets the job done). The primary difficulty is in photo setup, especially for product shots. Other kinds of shots primarily employed by businesses—photos of events, the business location, etc., come pre-built with a set, and this makes the resulting job that much easier.

When it comes to great product shots, you only need to do it once—be willing to spend money on hiring photographers to do an initial batch if you don't feel comfortable taking the photos yourself. If you are somewhat comfortable behind a camera, use the Peerspace app to find shoot locations. Great spaces run as low as $25 an hour, while fancier locations can run as much as $150 or more an hour. Little technical knowledge is required and using rented-out spaces like those on the next page is by far the most cost-effective way to access quality photo sets.

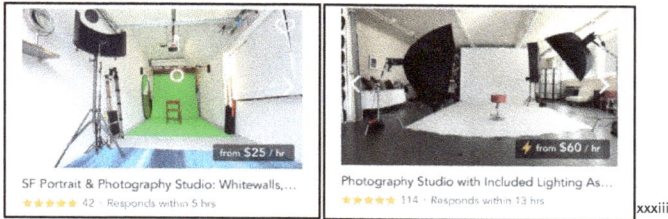

When taking any kind of photos related to a business, simplicity is usually better. Aim to stick to a general stylistic theme and color profile.

In the below abstract images, note the use of light, contrast, and focus.

In the below product images, note the simplicity of the backgrounds and color profiles.

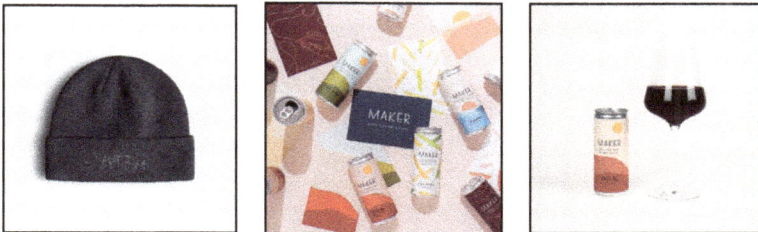

Again, while the barrier of entry to taking the type of photos most used by small businesses, such as product and location shots, event media, and team pictures are not incredibly difficult to create, it must be emphasized that visuals are incredibly important in the online space. It's far better to spend some additional money and hire an agency than it is to do it yourself if you do not feel comfortable working with cameras and sets.

In sum: as a business, put in the time, effort, and money required to look good. Such a strategy is eminently necessary for digital environments.

Video

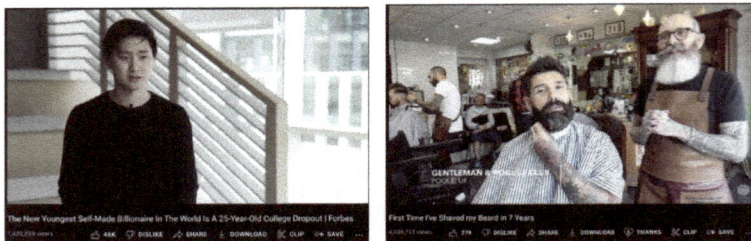

xxxv

Video is important for business since it's a very efficient way of communicating a vast amount of information to a viewer in a short amount of time (if one picture is worth a thousand words, what is a video worth?).

Whether you're creating short-form clips, longer YouTube videos, or video ads, knowing how to produce great videos at minimal cost is valuable.

Videography for business is best viewed as an extension of photography: keep it visually simple and don't feel the need to splurge on crazy sets or over-the-top edits (nor 4k resolution—1080p is just fine). Just keep in mind that you will need microphones (either on-body or on-camera gets the job done) in addition to a camera when filming videos.

If you're looking to make videos in-house, the same strategy of renting video sets through a service such as Peerspace is maximally cost-effective. Editing is best done through Adobe Premiere Pro or Final Cut Pro. DaVinci Resolve is a great free alternative.

On a final note, don't be afraid to outsource video production—just as with photography, it's how many people will be introduced to your business. It's much better to do it right at a higher cost—just don't subscribe to the notion that you can't do it right in-house, or outside a reasonable budget.

7

Automation & Sustainability

Most social media creators and managers fail to mention that *social media is hard*. Establishing an online presence is hard. Creating engaging content is hard. Building an optimized funnel is hard. They must be hard because the spoils of success are immense—as the adage goes, if it was easy, everyone would do it.

Thankfully, there are some tools that make running the digital aspects of your business easier. **Outsourcing** is bringing in other people, typically specialized workers, to run certain parts of the business. **Automation** is building out systems that run themselves. Nearly all aspects of social media and digital media can be outsourced or automated to the notable benefit of the business owner.

Today, outsourcing is done through a variety of services that connect you to specialized freelancers. These services are valuable for a few reasons: primarily, since they connect you to freelancers around the world and the field is so competitive on the supply side, you get access to a massive range of potential workers at low prices. In this manner, many of the menial tasks inherent to digital and social marketing are low-hanging fruit to be outsourced at relatively low cost. Of course, if you have willing labor to do the work in-person (again, interns are great for this), that is usually the better option, but for everyone else, outsourcing is the way to go. Here are some common tasks that are easily outsourced:

- Website creation.

- Trend research.

- Content ideation.

- Article and copywriting.

- PPC (pay-per-click) campaign management.

- Posting content.

It may feel strange to give a stranger access to parts of your business. Keep in mind that freelancers rely upon good reviews and word-of-mouth to generate clients; by only working with established freelancers (or agencies) presenting a strong history and review base, there is absolutely no security risk in outsourcing.

The primary difficulty in working with freelancers is that they are not as intimately familiar with the workings and brand strategy of your business as you and your employees are (this is why the most easily outsourced tasks are those requiring little actual knowledge of the business). There are several remedies to the issue—one, simply share resources that educate freelancers on your business and vision (this is much more realistic if freelancers are contracted for the long term), or two, work with an agency that puts an unusual degree of time and effort into understanding your business (simply put, find good freelancers and agencies to work with).

As for where exactly these freelancers can be found—consider the following list:

- **Fiverr:** Fiverr is the largest marketplace for freelancers and presents a wide range of offerings. It is the least vetted, but often the lowest-cost, service on this list.
- **Upwork:** Upwork is an industry leader in the freelancer space primarily focused on web dev, graphic design, writing, and marketing services. Upwork is great for establishing longer-term relationships and contracts.
- **Designhill:** specializes in graphic and web design services.
- **Toptal:** screens freelancers to offer only "the top 3% of freelance talent." Toptal focuses on services in the software development, design, and product management spaces.
- **Reedsy:** specializes in providing services to authors but is great for hiring any sort of editor or ghostwriter for blog, copywriting, or graphic design work.
- **99designs:** specializes in design services.
- **Codeable:** specializes in anything and everything related to WordPress.
- **Gun.io:** specializes in software engineering.
- **PeoplePerHour:** great for short-term projects.
- **Skyword:** concentrates on writing and content strategy.

If you would prefer to work with an agency, which is typically more expensive but provides a more personalized experience and a greater volume of services. You can find some local ones simply by searching "social media agency near me" or "digital marketing agency near me" on Google. Alternatively, find any number of agencies that operate digitally by searching up the tasks you're looking to outsource.

When it comes to outsourcing low-skill tasks, opt for the best price. For high-skill tasks, focus on quality over price.

Additionally, note that freelancer websites that require you to post a job and freelancers to compete for the spot often drive freelancers to bid significantly under their ideal rate. Take advantage of this process relative to sites like Fiverr where you view job listings posted by freelancers.

That's what you need to know when it comes to outsourcing—it's a powerful method to simplify and accelerate the digital marketing process (or really any business process for that matter) at any level or type of business.

The second way of doing those same things is automation—previously defined as the creation of systems that run themselves, automation is better viewed as the removal of human labor and effort from a process, typically through software and code. While outsourcing replaces in-house labor with out-of-house labor, automation is much closer to a one-time fix: once a human-dominated task is automated, it rarely goes back.

Automation is extremely prevalent in the digital space. Businesses incorporate software and automation into all types of important tasks, including not only those that humans once performed, but those that never could be done by human workers. Consider some aspects of digital marketing ripe for automation:

- PPC Management and Optimization (for example, ad spend adjustments as per performance rules)
- Social Media Engagement (dm auto-responders, auto-engagement)
- Posting (post scheduling)

The easiest type of automation to implement is SaaS, or software-as-a-service, which lets you pay a monthly subscription to use software that automates some aspect of your digital activities.

For example, I worked with Ivan at AdsDroid for some time to manage my Amazon ads. His software automatically identifies top-performing keywords and alters ad bids over time. In this manner, without coding anything yourself, you can leverage powerful software tools to automate digital workflows.

I'll list some popular digital automation services below, as well as their intended purpose:

- **Zapier**: custom automation across 5,000 apps.
- **Hootsuite**: schedule posts, monitor competition, and view unique analytics.
- **Later**: schedule posts and manage comments.
- **Tailwind**: scheduling and analytics tool, best for Pinterest.
- **CoSchedule**: mass post scheduler.
- **Iconosquare:** advanced analytics.
- **BuzzSumo**: identify trending topics and influencers.
- **Scoop.it**: curate content from other sources.
- **Mention**: see where your brand is mentioned, identify influencers, and monitor keywords in real time.
- **MeetEdgar:** build a library of content you'd like to share across different platforms and get it automatically scheduled and shared for you.
- **SocialPilot**: post scheduling, team collaboration, bulk upload, Facebook ad campaign management.

- **Facebook Pages Manager**: manage your Facebook pages.
- **Zoho Social**: scheduler and analytics tool, great for teams who collaborate digitally.
- **PromoRepublic**: local marketing platform.
- **Audiense Connect**: Twitter management.
- **Napolean Cat**: wide range of automation features for cross-platform campaigns.

Other tools can be used to manage digital collaboration, as follows:

- **Slack**: internal communication.
- **Asana**: collaborate on projects.
- **Trello**: organize your projects.

In sum, automation presents a second method to mitigating the costs (in terms of time and effort as well as money) of digital operations. Efficiency is the goal: since social media is a long-term game, eliminating the short-term work and creative effort put into social media and all types of digital operations while maintaining output best ensures the longevity and success of any digital endeavor.

8

Advertising

People and companies skilled at paid advertising essentially have access to a money printer. There is an excess of advertising channels available, ranging from Facebook and TikTok to Google and YouTube. Most ads are intended to sell a product or service, though some large companies run massive campaigns just to build brand goodwill. Good ads designed to sell a product or service are lifetime profitable; the profit accrued from the ads is greater than the ad spend not necessarily in the short-term but considering derived lifetime customer value (LTV).

Since paid advertising is so scalable and reaches so many hundreds of millions of people, breakeven or profitable adverts are an incredibly valuable tool. Of course, online advertising isn't a secret, and it isn't easy. Many ad operators operate at a loss to drive traffic and sales to their products in the hope that the paid marketing eventually builds organic momentum.

No matter the objective profitability of ad spend, a person with the ability to improve the effectiveness of a company's ads, no matter what that effectiveness is, is worth big dollars to that organization. A person who excels at paid advertising can drive enormous amounts of targeted traffic to websites of their choosing, and many individual entrepreneurs utilize this in their own pursuits.

So, what does paid advertising entail? Generally, advertising involves a funnel. Each advertising funnel has several stages, which introduce people to the brand and business at the top-most level, and turns them into paying customers at the bottom-most level. Funnels don't always need to funnel toward a purchase point, just toward the KPIs identified in the brand and social strategy sections. For example, consider the following funnel of a theoretical business:

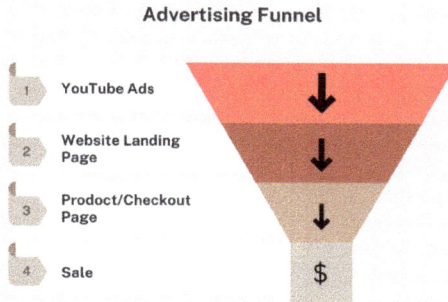

Advertising Funnel

1. YouTube Ads

2. Website Landing Page

3. Prodoct/Checkout Page

4. Sale

$

Creating great paid advertising funnels isn't just about the ads. Instead, each step of the funnel must be optimized to get as many people as possible to the next stage. In the theoretical case, let's say that 1 million people see the YouTube ad of a small business. Out of the 1 million, just 10,000 click on the ad and progress to the landing page. Then, just 1,000 progress to the product checkout page, and 100 convert into a sale. At any stage, a bad step in the funnel (say, a bad website, ad, or checkout page) could drastically impact results. In this manner, each stage must be worked on to ensure that the best possible overall funnel is created. Let's explore tips to create and improve each step of the funnel.

At the top of a paid advertising funnel is an ad, which gets shown to users of a given medium, such as a social networking website. Ads usually are the lowest-converting stage of the entire funnel since users are over-exposed to ads on most platforms. While the subject of ad creation will be explored thoroughly throughout the per-ad platform sections, focus on these key things across the board (and across all platforms) when creating ads:

Create with your audience in mind. You aren't creating an advertisement for everyone. You're creating ads designed to resonate with your audience (your future customers). Keep that group and their specific problems in acute focus.

Copywriting/speaking. Depending on the format (photo, video, text, etc.), you have a brief time in which to communicate a message to your viewers. In video ads, you must have a concise hook (depending upon length), while in photo and text-based ads, a catchy headline is imperative. Work on simplicity and incorporate the brand taglines identified in the brand strategy section. Ensure, above all, that if you were in the shoes of a potential customer, you would keep watching your own ad (ask some friends too—you may be a little biased).

Design (visuals). Visuals, or images, are dependent upon the type of advertisement you choose to produce. Video ads are visually different from graphics, or from text ads. When it comes to video ads, visuals and design elements should support and further the messaging and call-to-action. Think back to the brand strategy section and base design on those choices. Consider pacing and length—you want to produce just a 15-second video ad, or perhaps a longer 2-minute video. These choices will be considered in-depth throughout the YouTube ads section. For photo-based ads, it is even more critical that visual elements support the messaging and call-to-action of the ad. Keep it simple and on-brand.

Message. Beyond the initial hook, great product-focused advertisements clearly impart the value of their business and offering to viewers. Most identify or allude to a problem and describe the solution being offered, often in a manner that incorporates social proof. No matter the type of advertisements you produce, keep the messaging in mind, and keep it short and powerful.

Call-to-Action. Call-to-actions encourage customers to take the actions leading to your KPI. Call-to-actions may take the form of "buy now", "book a call", or "learn more." Whatever it is, ensure it's visually clear and direct. Consider offering some sort of incentive beyond the value proposition of the business, such as a discount, trial, or reward, and aim to increase urgency.

Following conversions derived from ads, customers are usually directed to a landing page of some sort. A landing page is a standalone web age created specifically for a marketing campaign. Alternatively, you can direct viewers to a social profile of your business on which you're looking to grow a following. The landing page typically funnels users to the final stage of the funnel, whether that's joining an email list, visiting the geographic location of a store, or buying a product online. When creating landing pages or websites, consider these best practices:

Clearly communicate a message. Most people will click off your landing page near-immediately. Your page must have a strong headline that concisely imparts the value of the page (why a viewer should stick around). You can use the tagline of your business or offer a discount. No matter how you do it, make sure someone in your target audience who has no prior exposure to your business will want to stick around.

Vibrant visuals and compelling copy. This ties into your brand strategy as a whole—ensure that the visuals (which are a must!) and the colors of the landing page communicate the vibe of the business. For example, if you're a personalized interior design agency, you may opt to go for light, friendly colors and images of happy clients and team members. If you offer operations consulting to corporate customers, you may utilize a darker and more refined color set with data-driven visuals. Additionally, ensure your headline is followed up by concise but powerful copywriting. Testimonials, photos with customers, and social proof visuals (anything that communicates you're real and professional) all work well.

Strong call-to-action. Your call-to-action drives viewers of the page to perform an action that pushes them further along your funnel. For example, "download", "get it now", and "book a call" are all call-to-actions. Ensure that the call-to-action on your landing page is clear and that all elements on the page lead viewers to it. You may offer some sort of discount or reward to encourage people to take the call to action.

Ensure that the call-to-action signup process is not difficult. Clicking on "book a call" and then having to fill out pages of personal information, for example, is sure to drastically reduce sign-up rates even once the call-to-action button is clicked. Rather, simplify and shorten the customer experience as much as is reasonably possible.

We've now explored the big-picture steps involved in creating a paid advertising funnel—first the ad, then the landing page, and finally the call-to-action and resulting behavior. We'll now progress into a description of the top ad platforms and the gritty best practices for each.

Google Ads

Google Ads is the quintessential search engine ad platform. It serves ads to the 70,000 people Googling something every second and to its four-odd billion users overall.

Google Ads average a click-through rate of 2%, meaning that one user in fifty clicks on a regular ad. 1.2 million businesses use Google Ads, while businesses make on average $2 in revenue per each ad dollar they spend.

Ad · https://www.nerdwallet.com/   ⋮
2022's Best Credit Cards - The Best Credit Cards of 2022
Find the **best** 0% APR, low interest, balance transfer, student, travel, and rewards **cards**. Expert reviews of all the **top**-rated **credit cards** on the market. We've found 2022's **best**. Low Interest Rates. Up to 5% Cash Back. Find the **Best Card**. Mobile-Friendly

Ad · https://experience.gm.com/my_gm_rewards/card   ⋮
My GM Rewards Card - Exclusive Perks & Benefits
15,000 Bonus Points Earned When You Spend $1,000 In Your First 3 Months. See Offer Details. Reward Yourself & Apply Now For A My GM Rewards **Card**. Start Earning Points Upon Approval. 0% Intro APR- Terms Apply. 7x Total Pts On GM Spend.

Ads · Shop investing books   ⋮

Rich Dad Poor Dad: 20th...	The Intelligent Investor Rev...	Fundamentals of...	How to Talk to Anyone -...	48 Laws of Power -...
$12.99	$14.29	$70.00	$16.95	$14.95
Was $25	Amazon.com	McGraw Hill	Was $25	Was $24
Audible.com			Audible.com	Audible.com

xxxvi

In sum, Google Ads is a powerful tool for all types of businesses. The platform is built upon a PPC, or pay-per-click, model. This means that you only pay when your ad is clicked on—if 1 out of 100 people click on the ad, you only pay for the one click, not the hundred views (known as impressions). Keep the following terms in mind not only when it comes to Google Ads, but all PPC ad platforms:

- A **keyword** is a word or phrase searched by users who see your ad.

- Click-through rate, known as **CTR** or **CTW**, is clicks divided by impressions, or the number of people who clicked on your ad versus the number of people who saw it (e.g., if one in one hundred people click on an ad, the CTR is 1%).

- A **bid** is how much you're willing to pay for each click. Ad platforms work like auction houses: given that many businesses are competing for the same keywords, only the ad with the highest bid gets the placement.[17]

- Your **CPC**, or cost per click, is the cost of ads divided by the number of clicks.

- **ROAS**, or return on ad spend, is equivalent to total conversion value (e.g., units sold, or customers generated) divided by total costs. It is similar in this manner to ROI, though keep in mind that it is based upon revenue divided by costs, not profit.

With these terms in mind, visit **ads.google.com** to get started with Google Ads. Note that Google gives $500 in free ad credit to first-time users who spend $500 on ads.

Once you sign up with your business email, follow a few brief setup steps. You'll arrive at the "now it's time to write your ad" page.

When writing copy, focus on keeping it simple. You have limited space, so think back to your target audience and message. Include a call to action, and make sure your ads line up with what viewers will experience when they click on the ad and progress down the funnel. Use social proof, and if you intend to advertise locally, make clear that you service a specific local area.

On the next page, choose specific and relevant keywords that you imagine someone interested in your product or service

---

[17] This is a simplification. Stick with it for now, but keep in mind that quality counts, not just bid price.

would search. Then, specify the locations in which you want your ad to show. If you're a business with a physical location, go hyper-local. If not, choose areas that most represent the demographic you're aiming at.

Finally, choose a reasonable budget (start small, but not small enough that results will be difficult to measure). Once you add payment info, you're ready to go! Just confirm that the $500 credit offer is applied to your account (viewable as you add payment information).

The Google Ads algorithm incorporates a quality score into bids. For this reason, new accounts and campaigns may take some time to get up and rolling—understand that this is Google figuring out the quality of your ad, not any fault of yours.

As you continue using Google ads, consider the following strategies and best practices:

- **A/B test headlines and descriptions.** The advertising game is all about testing as many ads and keywords as is reasonably possible, and sorting through them to identify the best performers. To do this, perform A/B tests by creating new ads that change just one variable of top-performing ads. For example, if targeting people in Canada with the search term "buy camera gear" is your top-performing ad, try advertising with that same keyword in the United Kingdom. Split testing in this manner over time, as well as layering on demographic and interest areas (on other platforms as well as Google), is the tried-and-true formula for long-term PPC success.

- **Eliminate low-performing keywords and locations over time.** By testing out lots of keywords and consistently removing the lowest-yielding ones, you'll build up to the most profitable, least-cost ads.

- **Advertise on competitors' keywords.** If people search for competitors that offer similar products or services to yours, they'll likely be interested in your products and services as well. So, simply add the names of your competitors as keywords that your ads will display on. When using this strategy, focus on what differentiates you from the competition in the headlines and descriptions.

Note how these strategies play out in a book promotion I'm currently running (below). The ad is operating at a low 1% CTR and a similarly low $0.05 CPC. Given that approximately 3% of clicks convert to a sale and the average profit derived from each sale is $3.5, the ad is generating a profit ROAS of 1.8, or $1.8 in gross profit per every dollar spent on advertising.

In addition to these overarching strategies, here are some tools that can help you to identify keywords and optimize ads:

- **SEMrush**: powerful keyword research and analysis.
- **SpyFu:** keyword tracking and competitor research.
- **Answer the Public**: see what people are searching.
- **ClickCease**: prevent click fraud and click farms.
- **Dashword**: optimize ad copy.

I'll conclude by restating that Google is the single-largest ad platform in the world by far, with billions of consumers clicking on its ads. Give it time and understand that profitability isn't just dependent upon luck when it comes to PPC success, but rather the work you put in to optimizing campaigns.

YouTube Ads

As the world's leading video-sharing site, YouTube logs over two billion unique visitors per month. Relative to text-based Google ads, YouTube lets you get in front of an audience in a highly visual—and if done right, engaging—manner.

Since Google owns YouTube, YouTube Ads can be setup on the Google Ads platform, and YouTube lets you advertise videos in Google search results.[18] We'll focus on video advertising within the YouTube platform.

YouTube Ads can be used to increase engagement and increase subscriber growth on a YouTube channel, or (as is more popular) to drive viewers down a funnel to ultimately engage with a given business. In the below campaign of mine, note the dirt-cheap

---

[18] As well as advertise text-only ads within YouTube.

CPV, or cost-per-view. Essentially, for about $100, this campaign was able to effectively 10x the average view count of the channel at the time, display the ad to nearly 300,000 people in the vicinity of the business behind the channel, and generate significant subscriber traction.

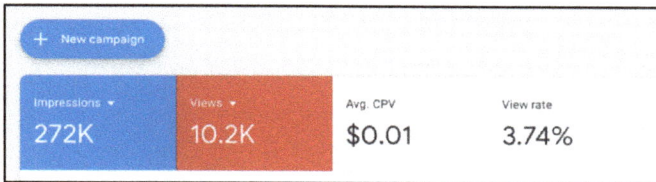

Alternatively, note the below campaign, which was designed to generate clicks and drive customers to a website. Either of these contrasting models, or some combination of the two, can be used as per your digital and social strategy objectives.

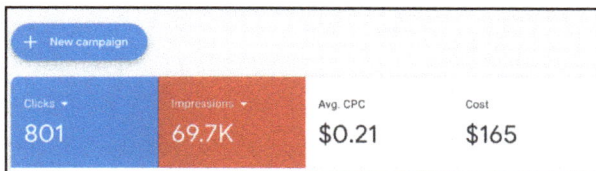

Now, note the different kinds of YouTube ads, as follows:

Skippable in-stream video ads: these ads play before (pre-roll) or during a video (mid-roll) and can be skipped after five seconds. As in the PPC model, you only pay if a viewer clicks on the ad or watches either the whole video (if sub-thirty seconds in length) or the first thirty seconds.

Non-skippable in-stream video ads: since most YouTube viewers automatically skip ads at the five-second mark, YouTube offers non-skippable in-stream ads. These ads, which can be up to 15 seconds in length, cannot be skipped by users, and play either before or during a video. However, YouTube charges for impressions for non-skippable ads, as opposed to per-click or per-view. So, the increased cost of non-skippable ads must be weighed against the increased engagement.[19]

Discovery ads: these ads show up alongside search results as opposed to before or during a video. As opposed to viewers directly watching the video, they have the option of clicking on it and being directed toward the associated video or channel. Discovery ads allow for three lines of text in addition to a video, and for this reason, are good for businesses with snappy copy (especially copy scripts that worked well on other ad platforms) and a lesser focus on the video-only approach.

To set up an initial campaign, sign into your Google Ads account or sign up at ads.google.com (note that the $500 credit on your Google ads account can also apply to YouTube Ads).

Click "new campaign." Choose a campaign objective, just as you would when setting up a Google ad, and when selecting campaign type, make sure to choose "video."[20] You may need to set

[19] There are also bumper ads, which are a form of non-skippable ads that are just 6 seconds in length. Given the length, bumper ads are best for brand reach and awareness campaigns, not for campaigns focused on reaching a local audience or selling a product.
[20] You may also directly reach the video ad setup page by Googling "youtube ads."

up conversion tracking, which is a simple website integration, depending on the objective you choose.

Then, select the campaign subtype (one of the ad types described above). Ignore "outstream" and "ad sequence" for now. Choose the language of the ad, the locations where you want to advertise, the campaign goal (going with the automatic selection is fine, and no need to set a target cost per action as a first-time user), and your budget.

You can now create a custom audience, which incorporates demographics, interest, and remarketing (e.g., users who have already engaged with your content or website). Design your custom audience around the target audience you defined for your business in the brand strategy section. Make sure not to be overly specific, or else the reach of the ad will be limited. As for placements—if you're new to online advertising, cast a wide net through a few dozen keywords, topics, and placements that fit your target audience. Google will do this for you based on the content of the video you advertise with, so you can also opt to leave placements as "any."

You may need to add content for a companion banner—if so, just let Google autogenerate it for you. Finally, make sure to choose a strong call-to-action and headline for display under the video advertisement.

You're now ready to click "create campaign." Your ad should start running within a few hours. Keep these strategies and tips in mind as you continue to operate YouTube Ads:

Ensure your **Google Ads account is linked to your YouTube channel**. To do so, click "tools and settings", "setup", and "linked accounts."

Set YouTube ads to unlisted. YouTube ads must be uploaded to YouTube. If you intend to use videos for ads but don't want them public on your main channel, just set the visibility to "unlisted" in the video settings. Additionally, download the YouTube studio and Google Ads apps for on-the-go analytics.

In a study by Unskippable Labs, **30-second skippable YouTube ads were found to have the highest view-through rate (VTR).** The first five or so seconds are the most important—focus an ad on the value proposition, pitch, tagline, or offer made in that initial timespan.

Design ads specifically for mobile or desktop viewing. Ads for mobile viewing should have large and clear text and graphical elements. Desktop allots more space for creative elements and design features.

Leverage campaign experiments. Campaign experiments (similar to A/B testing on Facebook, as is coming up) let users copy ads and change one or multiple variables. This lets you test how changing certain variables, such as keywords, landing pages, or audiences, affects ad performance.

Quality wins. So does authenticity. Quality and authenticity represent two contrasting approaches to advertisements—say, a Superbowl-feel advertisement with famous actors, complex sets, and visual effects versus a person recording on their iPhone 6 in their living room. Both themes work—take some time to think about what kind of overarching ad theme and style fits your brand and communicates with your audience in the best manner possible. Bringing in outside help to create great ads is nearly always the right move.

Learn from competitors, and from yourself. If competitors offering similar products or services to yours have been running YouTube ads for some time, they probably have something figured out. Use their ads as a data point when considering how to design your ads and campaigns. Additionally, if you've found success on other ad platforms, incorporate those learnings into your YouTube ad creation and optimization process. Your summed marketing activities (especially among digital ad platforms) are best viewed as a network that exponentially learns what works and what doesn't over time.

We've now covered YouTube ads—next up is the behemoth of social ads.

Facebook Ads

While Google may be the quintessential search engine (browser) ad platform, Facebook is the classic social media ad platform. Facebook has nearly three billion monthly active users, while the average conversion rate (CTR) of Facebook ads is right around 9%, and 41% of surveyed retailers said their ROAS was highest on Facebook. Facebook is also a powerful ad platform in that it provides a range of tools to let advertisers accurately target the people it seeks to reach, such as through interests, behaviors, history, and so on. While the targetability of Facebook ads has decreased in recent times because of privacy concerns, it still presents very powerful targeting tools relative to most major ad platform.

Facebook ads are integrated with Instagram (since Meta, formerly Facebook, owns both Facebook and Instagram) to the extent that ads created through Facebook can be run simultaneously on Instagram.

Finally, Facebook has a "Meta pixel" (formerly Facebook pixel) which is a piece of code added to your website. This lets you effectively track the actions that customers take through Facebook ads to better monitor conversions and bottom-line metrics. The Facebook pixel also lets you retarget customers later, as it tracks their actions once they visit your website and aggregates that data to automatically optimize ads. Pixels can even be set up on your website even before you start using Facebook ads.

To do so, go to "events manager" under "all tools" at business.facebook.com. Click "connect data sources", "web", and then select "Meta Pixel." Click connect, then give it a name and enter your website URL. You'll be able to automatically connect to WordPress. If you opted to use any other website provider than WordPress, search for a tutorial on how to manually install the pixel into that system.

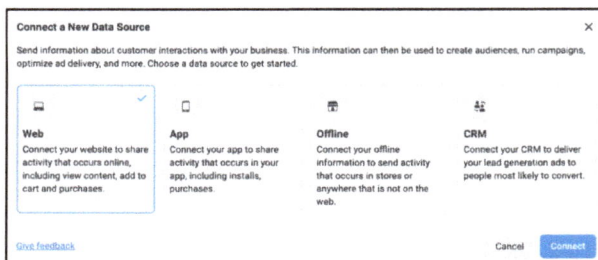

Once the pixel is integrated, you can set up events. Events are actions that people take on your website, like purchasing a product, joining an email list, or booking a meeting. While you can set up events manually, it's easiest to do so through the event setup tool, which can be found in the Meta Events Manager.

With the pixel properly installed and events created, let's explore the Facebook ad platform and campaign setup.

Confirm you're logged into your Facebook business account. Then, visit facebook.com/adsmanager/manage/campaigns, which brings you straight to the ads manager. Make sure to download the Meta Ads Manager app for mobile analytics.

Next, click the "create" button under campaigns and choose a campaign objective. Most small businesses opt for sales, leads, or awareness. Once chosen, you'll be redirected to the new campaign page. Facebook ads operate on the following three levels:

Campaigns define the top-level goals of your advertising, such as the objective, and make it easy to group different campaigns by their assigned purpose.

Ad sets are one level below campaigns and define a certain audience that advertisements are shown to. Here, you'll also set budget, schedule, and bids.

Finally, an **ad** is what customers see. At the ad level, you'll add text, visuals, and a call-to-action button.

| ▣ Campaigns | ▦ Ad sets | ▢ Ads |

So, each ad set can have multiple ads, and each campaign can have multiple ad sets. During setup, you'll be prompted to create one campaign, one adset, and one ad.

Back at the campaign setup screen, choose a name, keep "A/B test" off (as it's easiest to do this in the ads manager toolbar), turn on "advantage campaign budget" and press next.

Now, on the ad set creation page, you can define the audience you want to reach. Connect your pixel, turn on "dynamic creative", and set a budget. It's best to split your budget across many ads (to ultimately funnel down to the top-performing ads) as opposed to spending it all on one single ad.

Next, choose your audience. Audiences can be customized based on location, age, gender, connections, demographics, interests, languages, and behaviors. Again, ads are really about experimentation, so you should aim to test a variety of audiences over time. For now, customize the audience to the normal type of customer you serve. Don't feel the need to use all the targeting options—if your customer base isn't biased toward a certain gender, for example, simply leave it as "all genders." While it's usually better to keep the audience selection specific to begin with, make sure your chosen audience isn't too small. If not, you won't be able to generate enough impressions nor meaningful conversions. Keep "advantage detailed targeting" on and make sure to save the audience for further use and A/B testing. Leave "cost per result goal" blank for now.[21]

---

[21] As cost per result varies widely, so it's best to only set a goal after you've established a baseline.

You can now progress to the ad setup page. Ensure the connected Facebook and Instagram accounts are correct. Then, choose the format, and note that "carousel" is best to display multiple images or videos detailing your offerings or business.

Custom media PPC ads are best—as with YouTube ads, people notice quality graphics, photos, and videos. More importantly, nearly everyone will immediately scroll past bad ones. Focus on simplicity and attractive visuals. As always, make sure to incorporate elements of your brand strategy.

When designing your ad and writing copy, think about the value proposition of the ad—you need something so sticky or enticing that people are sure to investigate. This could be a big discount, a unique product, a local service, or a heart-wrenching message. Whatever it is, make sure it's made clear in the headline, primary text, and graphics. Ad specs are as follows:

- **Image ads**: Size: 1,200x628 pixels. Ratio: 1.91:1.
- **Video ads**: File size: 2.3 GB max. Thumbnail size: 1,200 x 675 pixels.
- **Carousel ads**: Image size: 1,080 x 1,080 pixels.
- **Slideshow ads**: Size: 1,289 x 720 pixels. Ratio: 2:3, 16:9, or 1:1.

Make sure to fill out the five possible options for headline and description text (again, work backward to identify top performers from a strong starting set). Don't go keyword heavy or attempt to sound overly clickbaity—just communicate your value.

Finally, choose a relevant call-to-action button. Once done, you've successfully built a campaign, ad set, and ad. All that's left is to click publish.

Follow the same strategy outlined in the Google Ads section of splitting your budget across several ads and adsets, removing bottom performers, A/B testing top performers, and continuing this process over time (or to the extent that best serves your business). To end off, here are some quick tips to consider:

- Create Facebook Canvas ads—while higher-effort to create, they're proven to increase engagement.
- Increase post visibility through the "engagement" objective.
- Leverage the "lookalike audience" tool.
- Choose to only place ads on desktop or mobile (whichever fits your funnel better).

This concludes Facebook ads. Note that privacy changes are forcing Facebook to update its tracking mechanisms often. This book will be updated every year to reflect current conditions as accurately as possible but understand that the setup process may differ over time.

Instagram Ads

Facebook Ads automatically display on Instagram. This section concerns the "promoted posts" feature on Instagram, which lets users promote Instagram posts as if they were ads. Instagram ads are a great way to increase exposure and rapidly gain a following on Instagram.

To promote posts, sign into a business (professional) Instagram account. Navigate to "ad tools" and tap "choose a post." Choose the post you want to promote—if you haven't yet hooked up your Instagram account to the Facebook page of your business, now's the time.

Then, set the goal of the ad, customize the audience you want to reach, and choose your budget. Your ad will start running shortly—stay up to date with analytics either through the analytics button on each post or the "ad tools" button.

If you have an Instagram shop attached to your page, you can tag your products in a post, and then boost that post to include them in an ad.

While Instagram ads are not as likely to deliver asymmetric results compared to platforms such as Google or Facebook, they are notably stable and consistent in the results they deliver, and as stated, a great way to increase exposure and grow a following.

Consider the analytics from a small-scale post promotion of mine. $200 in ad spend generated about 1,400 likes, 70 shares, and 5,881 profile visits, which converted to several hundred new followers. On a relatively small account, this was a great boost to the growth of the page and the exposure of the post.

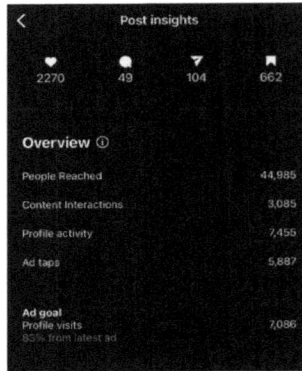

Unfortunately, Instagram does not currently offer rewards to first-time Instagram Ad users. If you would like a credit to create an ad through Facebook that could be shared on Instagram (without the engagement and exposure benefit of promoting a post), refer to the Facebook ads section.

We've now covered the main ad platforms: Facebook, Instagram, Google, and YouTube. We'll now explore a second tier of ad platforms: Nextdoor, TikTok, Pinterest, Snapchat, and Amazon.

Nextdoor Ads

This section was written with insight from Blake Martin, who used Nextdoor Ads to grow his curb painting business to six-figure profit as a high schooler.

Nextdoor is a powerful networking and lead-generation tool for businesses serving a local clientele. Featuring 70 million users, Nextdoor leverages community to help businesses grow—in fact, 88% of people shop at a local business at least once per week and

44% say they are willing to spend more at local businesses. So, leveraging Nextdoor as a megaphone to reach your local community through advertising and organic content is an absolute imperative for businesses with physical locations or serving a local community.

We'll examine several outreach techniques that are proven to have a beneficial effect on many small businesses. All businesses should set up their business page and share an initial post introducing their business on the Nextdoor platform; if your business offers low-ticket items and benefits most from a recurring local client base, regularly posting organic content is a prime strategy (relative to advertising, which we'll explore further on).

Within the initial post, follow either the *sell yourself* format or the *sell your client* method. The *sell yourself* method is classic, but effective all the same. Start by introducing your business to the community in a personable manner (incorporate your story as much as possible) and then state what differentiates you as a business relative to others within your community (include relevant visuals). As a first-line example:

"Hello, my name is Daegan. I'm a hairstylist in San Francisco specializing in solving hair loss."

Nextdoor has an older audience than the typical social media app, so Daegan stood out by providing a solution to a problem commonly found among older demographics. Replicating this within your Nextdoor pitch is dependent upon where you live— just analyze the age groups and demographics in your community.

Within the post, also include the pricing for your product/service and close with contact info and store location (if relevant), as well as discounts or rewards. You can think of this initial

Nextdoor post as being part of your funnel: the goal is to get people to engage with the post and follow through on the call to action.

The second post format, called the *sell your client* method, is all about getting your customer to consider the benefits they would experience from your products or services. For example, as opposed to Daegan simply describing his business, he could post a before and after photo of his hair loss treatment. By describing a regular customer and how he solves their problems, people who fit the target customer profile will react strongly—in essence, get the viewer thinking about what your product/service could do for them through visual cues, testimonials, and enticing language. Most importantly, make sure your posts tell a story. On Nextdoor, you don't want to sound like a generic advertisement, but at the same time, don't make your business sound like a hobby. Rather, tell a relatable, professional, and engaging story that ends with a call to action. Make sure to engage once you share the post—responding to comments goes a long way to strengthen connections.

In sum, you'd be surprised at the impact one strong Nextdoor post can have on your business. Apps like Nextdoor tend to exemplify the snowball effect—if your post blows up, everyone within a community will feel obliged to give your business a go, driven by FOMO and a desire to support local entrepreneurs.

Beyond organic content, advertising via Nextdoor is a powerful tool ideal for businesses selling high-ticket items or services. Note that Nextdoor ads do not run on a PPC model—instead, you pay upfront, and ads mix with organic content on the Nextdoor "home" tab. Since Nextdoor shows users relatively few ads relative to most other social platforms, conversions are usually better even if tracking and analytics are worse.

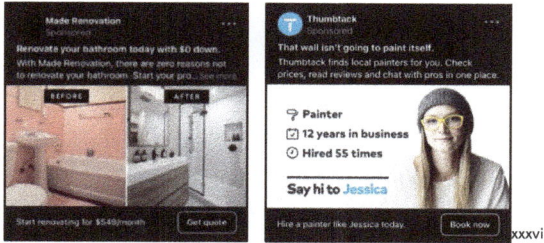
xxxvii

To get started, visit business.nextdoor.com. Click "claim your free business page" and make sure you're signed in with your personal Nextdoor account. Enter the name, address, and categories (choose multiple!) of the business. Upon clicking "create page" you will be directed to an ad creation page. Choose a goal for your campaign: "get more direct messages" is best for businesses selling high-ticket items or those built on lead gen, "increase website visits" is best for a business selling a range of products online, and "promote a sale or discount" is best, as may be guessed, when you have a strong sale or incentive to promote. Depending on the campaign goal you choose, complete the following step through one of two options:

Get more direct messages. Write some custom prompts detailing FAQs and questions potential customers are likely to ask. Fill out no less than three and no more than seven.

Promote a sale or discount & increase website visits. For ad content, focus on relatability and uniqueness. Identify top selling points and taglines from the brand identity section (for the headline), and use surveys, statistics, and testimonials as social proof (for the image). Ensure the click-through link goes to an optimized landing page and the call-to-action button fits with the landing page.

Then, consider the area you're looking to market your ads throughout. To do this, analyze where your current customers live, how they find you, and how far they'd be willing to drive for your product or service. Starting-uber local and expanding over time is usually the way to go.

Finally, set the budget, and click publish. Since Nextdoor ads are not based on a PPC model, upgrading and optimizing ad campaigns over time is largely a matter of running many, low-cost adverts ($3-$10 per day) and transitioning ad spend over time toward top performers.

Nextdoor really has done wonders for my business, and I'm a firm believer it can do the same for many businesses that rely on their local community to grow and thrive. Maybe your neighbor will be your best customer after all!

TikTok Ads

TikTok has recently taken the ad world by storm, and many online sellers are speaking of it as a gold rush. TikTok ads work best for businesses looking to target audiences under 30 years old with products or services that are offered online (e.g., don't try to advertise locally on TikTok). TikTok ads distribute across other apps in the TikTok network, notably Pangle and BuzzVideo.

All TikTok ads are short-form and vertically oriented; extremely short works best, so under the 15-second mark (though even shorter is often better). Visually appealing, as well as punchy messaging, is a must.

When setting up your first campaign, you'll be prompted under "create new" to choose the ad placements: you can either opt for auto-placement, where TikTok chooses for you, or go manual and select where you want your ads to show. It's initially best to either go with auto-placement or to test a wide variety of manual placements on a constrained budget. You can then build out custom audiences much as you would on Facebook (note that TikTok "ad groups" are equivalent to Facebook "ad sets"). Note that TikTok has a pixel similar to that of the Facebook pixel.

As a final note, I wouldn't recommend pushing TikTok videos as ads simply to increase exposure and grow a following. TikTok is just not difficult to grow on through organic content relative to nearly every other social platform and reaching anywhere near break-even through ads designed to increase exposure is implausible. I worked with one company that had been putting thousands of dollars into TikTok ads for that exact purpose—their account, despite being verified and having a large social team, ran itself into the ground and accumulated only a few hundred thousand likes, which translated into a sub-10k following and a near-complete loss in terms of ROAS.

Instead, leverage in-feed TikTok ads to encourage users to visit a landing page. Get going at getstarted.TikTok.com.

Pinterest Ads

Pinterest ads are best for companies with highly visual content and offerings, and often with some central theme of design. Most Pinterest ads are "promoted pins" which appear in feeds alongside regular pins. Promoted carousels are an engaging alternative to promoted pins. Pinterest has an equivalent of a Facebook pixel, called a Pinterest tag, so make sure to install it within your website prior to launching ad campaigns. Then, get started at business.pinterest.com, and make sure to follow the optimization practices outlined thus far.

Snapchat Ads

Snapchat ads are best for businesses selling their products or services online and looking to target younger demographics. Most Snapchat ads are short-form videos shown in-app that encourage users to swipe up and visit a link provided by the advertiser. These ads are just 3-10 seconds in length, so they must pack a significant punch in the brief time allotted. If Snapchat ads fit your business, think hard about how to crunch your messaging into a short-form video format. Get going at ads.snapchat.com.

Amazon Ads

Amazon ads can only be used by vendors to advertise the products they already have listed on Amazon. If you do have products listed on Amazon, consider incorporating Amazon ads into your digital strategy to boost product rankings and generate reviews, especially on newly launched products. Amazon offers several contrasting types of ads—sponsored products, sponsored brands, and video ads (video ads, notably, don't require you to advertise a product sold on Amazon). I recommend only leveraging sponsored product and brand ads if you sell products on Amazon—otherwise, stick to Google, Facebook, and YouTube advertising for products and services not sold through Amazon. In doing so, note that Amazon uses a similar PPC model to the platforms examined thus far. Simply follow those best practices and visit advertising.amazon.com to get started.

Here's what a day of an optimized Amazon ad campaign looks like (selling a $9 or so product):

Spend ⓘ	×	Sales ⓘ	×	Impressions ⓘ	×	Clicks ⓘ	×	ACOS ⓘ	×
$31.14 TOTAL		$101.50 TOTAL		34,582 TOTAL		63 TOTAL		30.68% AVERAGE	

Here's that same campaign when it first started running:

Spend ⓘ	×	Sales ⓘ	×	Impressions ⓘ	×	Clicks ⓘ	×	ACOS ⓘ	×
$33.38 TOTAL		$17.98 TOTAL		47,731 TOTAL		52 TOTAL		185.65% AVERAGE	

LinkedIn Ads

LinkedIn ads are best for B2B companies (businesses selling products or services to other businesses) and those selling professional products or services.

To get started with LinkedIn ads, click on "advertise" in the dotted box on the top right-hand of the homepage. Set up a

campaign manager account and click "create" and "campaign."[22]
Make sure to set up the LinkedIn Insight Tag (equivalent to the
Facebook Pixel) over time.

Follow a similar setup process to the ad platforms described
prior. To those interested in increasing LinkedIn engagement,
choose "video views" or "engagement" as campaign objectives. To
build out a funnel designed to sell a product or service, choose
"website conversions" or "lead conversions." Choose an ad format
based on the content type you've found, or feel, to be most effective
for your business. This could be video, images, or purely text-based
messaging. When completed, click "next" and fill in ad content. Then,
launch, and you're ready to go. Consider these tips as you continue
running LinkedIn ads:

- When working with small budgets, test a multitude of uber-
specific custom audiences (with target audiences of 50,000
as a minimum) with targeting you think will work best or
has worked well on other platforms.
- Leverage the performance chart and demographics tab to
adjust ads over time.
- Set up matched and lookalike audiences to re-target
website visitors. Find matched audience options on the
targeting screen in campaign manager and find lookalike
audience options under "plan", "audiences", and "create
audience."

---

[22] Note that LinkedIn campaign groups are simply one level of bucketing above
campaigns and exist purely for organizational purposes.

In sum, LinkedIn is a masterful platform for reaching professional audiences: use it well.

Niche Site Ads

Thus far, we've covered most of the world's largest ad networks. Remaining are all the niche players in the ad game—namely, those who offer ads on platforms focused on a single interest or demographic.

For example, my publishing agency routinely runs ads on Goodreads, which is a social platform specifically for readers.

To find niche ad opportunities, consider the websites and apps frequented by your target audience. Visit them and see if they offer ad placements. Just know that many smaller platforms have minimums—Goodreads, for example, requires a minimum of $5,000 in ad spend ($3,200 if working through a partner agency). If terms aren't clear, don't hesitate to reach out to support or admin teams.

Alternative Advertising

PPC advertising does not reflect the full range of digital advertisements nor marketing opportunities available. We will explore the two alternative strategies most employed by small businesses: influencer marketing and affiliate marketing.

Influencer Marketing

It has been made abundantly clear thus far that content creation is a lucrative opportunity for businesses to reach more people and turn those viewers into customers.

Influencer marketing yields a similar benefit to audience-building but circumvents the difficulty inherent in creating and sharing content: it involves businesses paying money or offering free products to social media influencers in return for advertisements to the audience of the influencer.

For example, a beauty brand may pay a beauty influencer with 500k subscribers on YouTube $3,000 to talk about the products of the beauty brand for thirty seconds within a video. Alternatively, the influencer may also receive $3,000 of free product in return for the advertisement or declare herself as being "sponsored" by the beauty brand and thus maintain a long-term relationship where the brand pays the influencer to use and advertise their products or services over the long-run and throughout the entirety of their social presence and content body.

As someone who's been both the influencer and the business in the influencer marketing relationship, I can speak to the win-win nature of influencer marketing and the fact that it's a viable strategy for practically all businesses, as influencers represent all niches and follower counts imaginable. To identify the influencers your brand can work with, explore these platforms:

- Influencity
- Upfluence
- Creator.co

Alternatively, search up your niche or industry on any given social platform, and check out the top influencers. Aim to work with influencers who have audiences that reflect your target demographics, high engagement rates, low advertisement counts, and values that fit with your brand.

When outreaching to influencers, personalized messages are best. Compare two emails I've received:

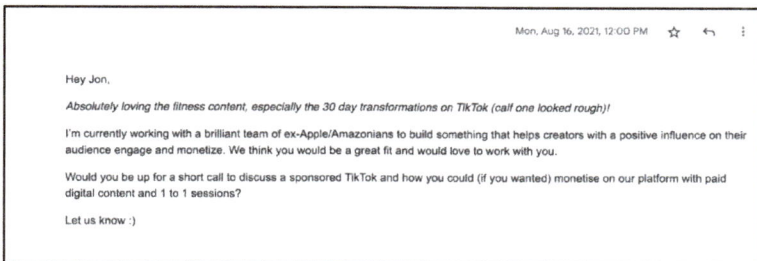

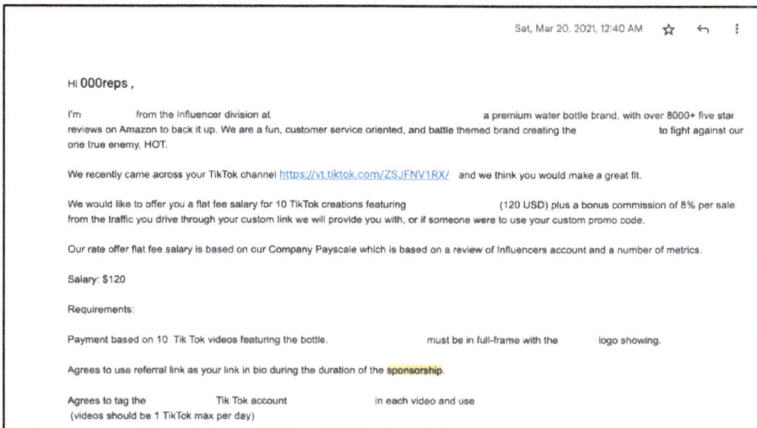

The top email showed that the writer had at least viewed some of my content prior to reaching out. The pitch was concise and the call-to-action was personalized and clear. This is everything you should do when reaching out to influencers. The second email is everything your outreach shouldn't have—an obviously automated and misspelled first line, painfully elongated text formatting, a fake name and blank profile picture, and a weak tagline ("our one true enemy, HOT" is just not the move, sorry guys).

So, while it may take some extra time to properly personalize outreach to influencers, it's more than worth it in the response it incurs. Outreach over email is usually best—if an influencer doesn't have one listed, reaching out through direct message is fine.

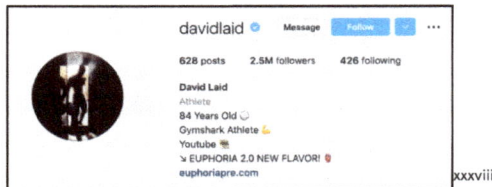

gymshark ✔   Message   Follow ∨   ...

4,175 posts   5.8M followers   128 following

Gymshark
if you're reading this you should go to the gym • •
gym.sh/NewReleases

jamal_b15 ✔   Message   Follow ∨   ...

1,147 posts   303K followers   799 following

Jamal Browner
B.S. Health and Human Performance
@gymshark athlete
@thegblbrand code "Jamal"
linktr.ee/Jamalb15

davidlaid ✔   Message   Follow ∨   ...

628 posts   2.5M followers   426 following

David Laid
Athlete
84 Years Old ☺
Gymshark Athlete 🦈
Youtube 📺
↘ EUPHORIA 2.0 NEW FLAVOR! 🧪
euphoriapre.com

xxxviii

Gymshark is one brand that powerfully utilizes influencer marketing. In fact, being sponsored by gymshark is viewed as an end-all status symbol in the bodybuilding and fitness community—influencers vie for Gymshark's attention in the hopes of receiving a sponsorship.

This is influencer marketing at its best, and Gymshark grew into a billion-dollar brand as a result.

Once you've outreached with influencers you think would work well with your brand for influencer marketing, all that's left is to verify that the influencer follows through on their side of the bargain. Aim to measure results, and only continue working with an influencer if they prove to produce more customers and profit for your business than they cost. If they perform unusually well, offer them a longer-term sponsorship.

Finally, note that influencer marketing goes a long way in helping your business grow an audience on social media—one mention from an influencer you're working with can easily 10x a small brand profile.

So, keep influencer marketing in mind as an immensely valuable tool to get the benefits of a social audience without having to build it yourself, as well as a route to speedrun the social growth of your business.

Affiliate Marketing

As our second form of alternative digital advertising, affiliate marketing is the process by which an "affiliate" or third-party earns a commission for selling your products or services for you. Affiliate marketing is most prevalent within the influencer community, since creators can easily capitalize upon their large audiences through affiliate commissions. Businesses, on the other hand, love affiliate marketing as it incentivizes other people to go about the hard work of selling their products and services for them.

For your business, set up an affiliate marketing program by simply designating unique codes to affiliates (really, to any user, as there's no downside to offering each account holder a code), who can automatically receive commissions to their account when customers check out using their code. This is easily done through the AffiliateWP plugin in WordPress (Pretty Links and Easily Affiliate also work). Some businesses, especially those with digital info products, can benefit by listing on clickbank.com, which is a marketplace for businesses and affiliate marketers.

Note these companies, which have created immensely profitable affiliate programs:

TradingView Partner Program

Earn money with the cutting-edge financial platform

Lifetime Profit

Receive a 30% commission
for all payments that your
referrals make

A 90-Day Cookie

Referrals that sign up within
90 days will be assigned
to you forever

Referral benefit

Your referral will get up to
$30 to put towards their new
plan

Start Earning

You've outdone
yourself.

Calling all publishers, creators, and
bloggers. Join our affiliate program to
monetize your content and connect with
the broader Robinhood community.

Apply now

US | Affiliate

Binance.US Affiliate
Program

Earn rewards when you introduce your community to crypto. Get up to $1,000 for
every referral. See program terms below.

Become an Affiliate

xxxix

In sum, both affiliate marketing and influencer marketing are
valuable digital strategies for all types of businesses. Each leverages
the power of other people—whether famous influencers or college
students sharing links amongst themselves—to grow your business
for you.

9

Back to Strategy

I'll impart the importance one final time of incorporating metrics and a data-driven approach into digital and social advertising.

Throughout the past eight chapters, we have examined a variety of tools imperative to the world of digital business—social strategy, social presence, content creation, PPC advertising, influencer marketing, and so on. A common thread throughout is the pursuit toward optimization: no funnel, advertising campaign, nor content pipeline will perform up to its full potential from day one, and online success for small business is largely a reflection of the degree to which data is measured, analyzed, and used as an engine toward further activity. Keep this tenet central to your digital operations moving forward.

By that same rule, let data govern decisions, not this book. We have done our very best to provide a comprehensive framework for businesses looking to enter social and digital spaces. This does not mean all businesses can benefit to the same extent from a given digital strategy or tool. Rather, each business is unique, and advice presented herein is best viewed as an underlying process, methodology, and knowledge base from which to operate.

The book can only end where it began: upon an introduction to a world increasingly defined by online interaction, and a business environment making its largest shift in history toward a massively globalized and digitalized system.

This future does not have to be scary—you are now equipped with the tools to embrace it and use it to further your message, products, and services.

As stated in chapter two, this book is first being published in fall 2022. A new edition will be released each year to reflect the rapidly changing fields and opportunities it explores. It will additionally evolve as per feedback delivered by actual readers. To give us the gift of your experiences, or to ask questions, reach out at team@smmfsb.com.

Appendix

What should you read next?

Thank you for reading this book! If you're looking for related reads and would like to support independent publishing, check out two of our popular works, *The Modern Guide to Stock Market Investing for Teens* and *Crypto Technical Analysis*.

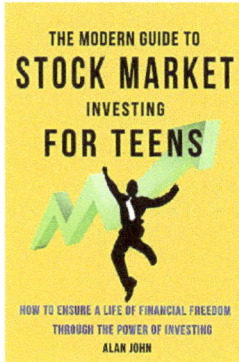

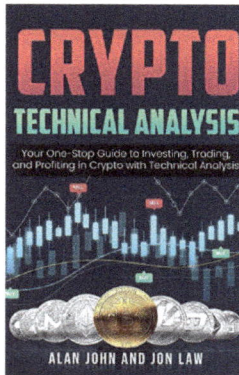

Acknowledgments

Following an aggressive year of writing in 2021 hallmarked by the publication of two books, I will admit that these past months have been less adorned. Getting back in the saddle was no easy task, though certainly a rewarding one. The credit is due to my wonderful team and people around me—starting with Will Warren for planting the seed that became this book and ending with the publication team at Aude.

Proper acknowledgments must begin at a much earlier time. This book and the knowledge within is the summation of wild entrepreneurial ventures throughout the many aforementioned fields. For the gift of those years, I extended my deep thanks to Jeremy Vaughn, Michael Thompson, Sreekar Kuckibhatla, Sharon Kha, Ben Wanzo, John Corcoran, Kai Lu, Jack Jacobs, Omar Rezec, Mahmood, and the many others I've had the pleasure of working with.

Thanks to Blake Martin and Ksenia Suglobova for valuable contributions to this text, as well as Dean Liang, Genesis Nguyen, and Jack Zimmerman for contributions to recent works.

My gratitude goes to Alyssa Callahan and Patchen Homitz— what pays, after all, but a seat of learning. On an equal note, a tribute is long overdue to Gil, Habeeb, Connor, Joyce, Justin, Malcolm, Malia, and all of Starroyo. My best wishes to everyone in the future.

Finally, dear reader, thank you for your time and thought. All books are for their readers—I hope this text has done you justice.

Resources

Services mentioned throughout the book.

Social Presence

Google.com/business

facebook.com/pages/creation

trends.pinterest.com

search.google.com/search-console

trends.pinterest.com

Slack

Asana

Trello

Zapier

Hootsuite

Later

Tailwind

CoSchedule

Iconosquare

BuzzSumo

Scoop.it

Mention

MeetEdgar

SocialPilot

Facebook Pages Manager

Zoho Social

PromoRepublic

Audiense Connect

Napolean Cat

Fiverr

Upwork

Designhill

Toptal

Reedsy

99designs

Codeable

Gun.io

PeoplePerHour

Skyword

Canva

Photoshop

Photopea

Mailchimp

Constant Contact

Drip

Hubspot

Sendinblue

SEMrush

SpyFu

Answer the Public

ClickCease

Dashword:

SEMrush

SpyFu

Answer the Public

ClickCease

Dashword

Advertising

business.pinterest.com

studio.youtube.com

ads.google.com

business.facebook.com

facebook.com/adsmanager/manage/campaigns

business.nextdoor.com

getstarted.tiktok.com

advertising.amazon.com

clickbank.

Domain, Website, & Hosting

godaddy.com

godaddy.com/en-in/hosting/WordPress-hosting

bluehost.com/WordPress

Squarespace

Weebly

Wix

Index

A fortiori.

| | | | |

Visuals

[i] *Google Business Profile, Morton's.*
[ii] *Google Business Profile, Proving Ground Waterfront Dining.*
[iii] *Instagram: B&N Supplements, Lucky's Markets.*
[iv] *Instagram: Philz Coffee, AgenciFlow.*
[v] *Instagram: Bay Club, Urban Remedy.*
[vi] *LinkedIn: Maker Wine*
[vii] *LinkedIn: Bitchin' Sauce*
[viii] *Pinterest: Boohoo*
[ix] *Pinterest: jewelry1000.com*
[x] *Pinterest: Ultra Beauty*
[xi] *YouTube: Mint.com*
[xii] *YouTube: Reign*
[xiii] *YouTube: MonsterInsights*
[xiv] *Tiktok: Bitchin' Sauce, TomoCredit, Yahoo Finance*
[xv] *Twitter: Sam Parr*
[xvi] *Twitter: Shaan Puri*
[xvii] *Wordpress.org*
[xviii] *GoDaddy.com*
[xix] *Coinbase.com*
[xx] *Hubspot.com*
[xxi] *Facebook: TomoCredit*
[xxii] *YouTube: NerdWallet*
[xxiii] *YouTube: Manscaped*
[xxiv] *YouTube: NewRetirement*
[xxv] *All YouTube [Analytics]: Ksenia Suglobova*
[xxvi] *YouTube: Alex Hormozi, Biaheza, Jordan B. Peterson, Mr. Beast, Nick Bare, Lost LeBlanc, Marie Forleo, Magnus Midtbo, Valuetainment.*
[xxvii] *YouTube: Jordan Welch*
[xxviii] *YouTube: BeardBrand*
[xxix] *LinkedIn: Arcade*
[xxx] *LinkedIn: Foundation Marekting.*
[xxxi] *Instagram: TomoCredit, Mosdotcom, The Economist*
[xxxii] *Instagram: Penguin Publishing, Portnum & Mason, David Yurman*
[xxxiii] *Peerspace app*

[xxxiv] *makerwine.com and shop.tesla.com*

[xxxv] *Forbes and Beardbrand*
[xxxvi] *Google.com*
[xxxvii] *Nextdoor: Made Renovation, Thumbtack*
[xxxviii] *Instagram: Gymshark, Jamal)b15, David Laid*
[xxxix] *TradingView, Robinhood, Binance.us*

All Non-Credited Social Analytic & Ad Visuals Owned by Jon Law

www.ingramcontent.com/pod-product-compliance
Lightning Source LLC
Chambersburg PA
CBHW040926210326
41597CB00030B/5187